Welcome to

2004

LET'S GO WITH THE CHILDREN

This edition has been researched and written
by

Janet Willsher

Thank you for helping Great Ormond Street Hospital Children's Charity in 2004, the centenary of the first ever production of Peter Pan.

Celebrating 00 Years of Peter Pan

The rights of Peter Pan were bequeathed by JM Barrie to GOSH. The value of this fantastic legacy remains a secret, at Barrie's request, in keeping with the magic and mystery of Peter Pan.

Through the sales of these guides we will have raised over £30,600. Since 1998 we have contributed to the funding of a mobile X-ray unit, syringe pumps, infusion pumps and a hoist, but this year we are committed to helping with a much bigger project tackling the hospital infrastructure. This 10-year redevelopment programme will upgrade the Hospital and increase its overall size enabling treatment for over 20% more patients. In the pursuit of excellence, the plan will bring the hospital right up to date with modern day medical practices and clinical care.

Funds contributed in 2004 will go towards the first stage of the re-development. A brand new Patient and Accommodation Centre, opening in 2004, will include 30 rooms for children who require short-stay treatments, along with their families. It will also contain eight transitional care flats for children who are well enough to leave their wards but need some care before they are allowed to return home.

We are proud to announce that a 6p contribution to the above charity will be made for each 'Let's Go with the Children' book sold this season. Thank you for your support. Registered charity No. 235825 ©1989 GOSHCC. ® 2003 GOSHCC

Getting yourself involved

Great Ormond Street Hospital Children's Charity needs everyone's support as they aim to raise over £20 million each year. There are many ways to get involved from trekking in Namibia to attending musical concerts. Log on to www.gosh.org or call 0207 916 5678 for an up to date listing of planned events, some of which can involve the whole family. Look out particularly for special Peter Pan themed events throughout the year.

Published by **Cube Publications**, 290 Lymington Road,
Highcliffe, Christchurch, Dorset BH23 5ET
Telephone: 01425 279001 Fax: 01425 279002
www.cubepublications.co.uk
Email: enquiries@cubepublications.co.uk
17th edition
ISBN 1 903594 43 X

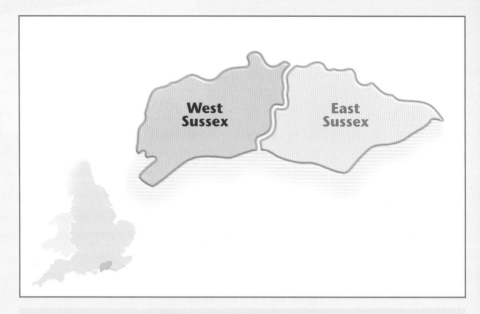

West
Sussex

East
Sussex

How to use this guide

This guide is one of a set of 13 covering all the counties of England and each county in this edition is colour coded as shown on the map above.

There are several chapters of subject interest as listed in the Contents opposite enabling you to choose something specific for you and your children to do or somewhere for you all to go.

If you have young children who love animals, dip into the Farms, Wildlife & Nature Parks chapter, or, if you have active teenagers, take a look at the Sports & Leisure chapter where you will find something to keep them busy.

Check out History, Art & Science and widen young horizons or choose a nearby venue from the Free Places chapter. A surprising number of things are free.

Whatever your budget, plan a day out to include a variety of activities. You may like to hire a boat, take a train ride, visit a really interesting museum, go bowling, stop off at a soft play centre, try snow sports, visit a zoo or go for a hike. Whatever interests you and your family, there is information included within the following chapters to help you occupy a wet afternoon, a long weekend or the whole school holidays.

We have highlighted price bands, facilities for school trips, places that are open all year and places that cater for birthday parties, but please call in advance if you have special needs or want particular information.

Whether you live locally or you are just visiting, you will find an amazing wealth of diverse interests, entertainments and activities in this area for children of all ages. We hope you will discover more about the area than you thought you already knew.

Please write to us with any constructive comments on the guide. We shall be delighted to hear from you. Our address is on page 1.

Use this guide with a good geographical map to help you find your way. Discover somewhere new, plan your route and keep the children busy by encouraging them to help with the navigating.

Contents

Key

Price codes are given as a maximum entry cost for a family of four, (2 Adults, 2 children):
A: £10 **B**: £20 **C**: £30 **D**: £40 **E**: £50 **F**: FREE **G**: Over £50 **P**: Pay as you go

Schools	School party facilities, visits by arrangement
Birthdays	Birthday parties are organised here
NT	National Trust property - www.nationaltrust.org.uk
EH	English Heritage property - www.english-heritage.org.uk
Sussex Past	www.sussexpast.co.uk

Telephone Numbers are provided for most entries.

Should you require special facilities for someone with a disability, please call before your visit to check suitability.

Opening Times

LAST ADMISSIONS
Many last admission times are an hour before the quoted closing time. If in any doubt, phone and ask if you know you will be arriving late. Don't get caught out and be disappointed!

WINTER AND CHRISTMAS OPENING
Many attractions close earlier in Winter and most are closed over Christmas and New Year. If you want to visit in this period, call in advance to check! At the time of going to print not all opening times were decided. We have suggested you phone for opening times if this was the case!

Look what you can do!

Drusillas p33

Volks Railway p31

Michelham Priory p18

Holmbush Farm World p37

Look what you can do!

Fishers Farm Park p38

Paradise Park p41

Knockhatch Adventure Park p39

Partytank p47

Horsham Visitor Attractions

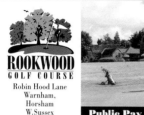

ROOKWOOD
GOLF COURSE
Robin Hood Lane
Warnham,
Horsham
W.Sussex
RH12 3RR
(off the A24 at Robin Hood roundabout)
Tel: 01403 252123

Public Pay & Play Golf at its Very Best...

18 hole Course – 9 hole Pitch & Putt – Golf Centre
Golf Shop – Lessons – Bar & Restaurant

Southwater Country Park

This 54 acre park offers a perfect mix of beautiful wildlife habitats and recreational opportunities including non-motorised watersports, fishing and adventure style play area.
Open daily with access for all.
Visitor centre, cafe. Admission free

Well signposted off the A24
For further information call 01403 731218

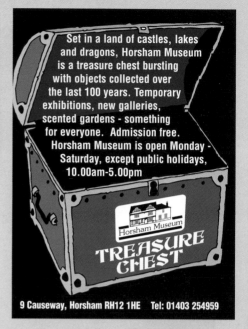

Set in a land of castles, lakes and dragons, Horsham Museum is a treasure chest bursting with objects collected over the last 100 years. Temporary exhibitions, new galleries, scented gardens - something for everyone. Admission free. Horsham Museum is open Monday - Saturday, except public holidays, 10.00am-5.00pm

Horsham Museum

TREASURE CHEST

9 Causeway, Horsham RH12 1HE   Tel: 01403 254959

THE PAVILIONS in the Park

Fantastic new Leisure Complex in the beautiful surroundings of Horsham Park. Features include state-of-the-art health and fitness suites, indoor and outdoor all year round heated swimming pools with flume ride, bubble beds, moving water channels, multi sports halls, adventure play areas, créche facilities and more!

For further information contact:
01403 219200

Leechpool & Owlbeech Woods

85 acres of beautiful ancient woodland, conifers and heathland. Two self guided trails and a surfaced path offers access for all. Open daily. Admission free.
Harwood Road (B2195),Horsham
For further information contact:
Tel: 01403 731218/256890

Warnham Nature Reserve

This tranquil reserve hosts a historical hammerpond, reedbeds, woodland and meadow. Open Thursday to Sunday throughout the year. Facilities include a nature trail, bird hides and a visitor centre. Cafe open at weekends during the Summer and on Sundays during the winter. Admission free.

Warnham Road (B2237), Horsham, W. Sussex
Tel: 01403 256890

Awarded for excellence

Horsham District Council
www.horsham.gov.uk/leisure

Another leisure service from

Horsham District Council

USEFUL INFORMATION

LOCAL COUNCILS

The Local Councils have Leisure Services Departments looking after a wide range of leisure facilities, many of which are featured within this guide, from the best parks and open spaces to sports facilities and museums. They may be able to provide further information on special events and playschemes organised for children, particularly in the school holidays.

EAST SUSSEX: Brighton and Hove: 01273 290000. Eastbourne: 01323 410000. Hastings: 01424 781066. Lewes: 01273 471600. Rother: 01424 787878. Wealdon: 01323 442666.

Hastings and St Leonards. Think of the grace and elegance of an original fishing boat as it sets out to sea. The dark romance of living on your wits and smuggling by moonlight. The song of the past whistling through the remains of a conqueror's castle. The wild, endless spectacle of an unspoilt country park. Take your children and see if you can discover the magic that lingers in the many attractions here. To find out what a minute, an hour, a day or a week might be like, visit www.visithastings.com or telephone for a free brochure, 0800 18 1066, ref. 2056. **Check out page 8.**

WEST SUSSEX: Adur: 01273 263000. Arun: 01903 737500. Chichester: 01243 785166. Crawley: 01293 528744. Horsham: 01403 215100. Mid Sussex: 01444 458166. Worthing: 01903 239999.

Horsham District Council , www.horsham.gov.uk 01403 215100, has a large variety of places of interest and visitor attractions to ensure wonderful days out. From Southwater Country Park, with its wildlife habitats and adventure play area, fishing, sailing and other recreational opportunities, to Leechpool and Owlbeech Woods offering two self-guided trails through ancient woodland and heathland. Warnham Nature Reserve provides a relaxing opportunity to view a large array of birdlife or to go on a nature trail. The Pavilions in the Park, the exciting Leisure Complex in beautiful Horsham Park, has much to offer with indoor and outdoor heated pools, a multi sports hall, adventure play areas and health and fitness suites. A visit to Horsham Museum, set in a land of castles, lakes and dragons, has something for everyone, with fascinating galleries and a scented garden. Horsham provides the visitor with every amenity and Rookwood Golf course has one of the best public 18 hole courses as well as a Pitch and Putt course. **Check out 'Free Places' and 'Adventure' chapters and page 6.**

TOURIST INFORMATION CENTRES

Tourist Information Centres are a great complement to this guide and can provide advice and detail on the many interesting local events that take place and local accommodation for visitors, as well as stocking colour leaflets about many of the attractions featured in this guide.

EAST SUSSEX: Battle: 01424 773721. Bexhill On Sea: 01424 732208. Boship: 01323 442667. Brighton and Hove: 09067 112255. Eastbourne: 01323 411400. Hastings: 01424 781111. Lewes: 01273 483448. Rye: 01797 226696. Seaford: 01323 897426.

WEST SUSSEX: Arundel: 01903 882268. Bognor Regis: 01243 823140. Burgess Hill: 01444 238202. Chichester: 01243 775888. Fontwell: 01243 543269. Horsham: 01403 211661. Littlehampton: 01903 713480. Midhurst: 01730 817322. Petworth: 01798 343523. Worthing: 01903 210022.

Please mention this guide when visiting attractions.

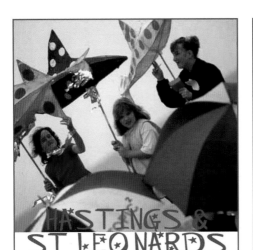

Sports & Leisure

Sport is a great way for young people to channel surplus energy or occupy spare time. It can offer personal challenges, foster team spirit and generate an interest, which can provide a pleasurable and necessary diversion in later life. Sport is a good way to have fun, make new friends, to be fit and feel good. Try ice-skating, snow sports, or the many different activities on offer at your sports and leisure centre.

Leisure pursuits may lead to a new hobby or simply occupy leisure time in a relaxed and entertaining way. Try pottery painting, take a language course or visit your local theatre.

Abbreviations: C: Canoeing, JS: Jet Skiing, K: Kayaking, PB: Power Boating, RB: Roller Blading, RBd: Raft Building, RS: Roller Skating, S: Sailing, SB: Skate Boarding, SDv: Scuba Diving, Sn: Snorkelling, Tu: Tubing, W: Windsurfing and Boards, WS: Water Skiing.

ADVENTURE ACTIVITIES

EAST SUSSEX: Flimwell, **Arena Pursuits,** www.arenapursuits.com 01580 879614, situated on the Kent/Sussex border, just off the A21, approx 21 miles from Jn 5 of the M25. The Centre offers 6-18s a range of exciting, fun activities that develop initiative, teamwork and leadership skills. The programme of outdoor activities includes junior half-day sessions (6-13) and Adventure Parties (10-16) offering obstacle courses, team challenges, treasure hunts and various woodland based adventure games. For older children (13+) there is a series of challenging team tasks. Full safety equipment is provided for Junior Paintballing (11+) and adult marshals strictly control this event. Other activities include Survival Parties (10+) and an Early Learning Driving programme (11+). All events are for pre-booked groups and ideal for schools, youth groups, scouts, guides and birthday parties. Schools Birthdays **Check out page 8.**

WEST SUSSEX: Chichester: **Cobnor Activities Centre** 01243 572791.

ADVENTURE HOLIDAYS

PGL Activity Holidays, www.pgl.co.uk 08700 507 507, has ten UK residential centres, offering activity holidays for 7-10, 10-13 or 13-16 year olds covering football, drama, kayaking, 'Adrenaline Adventure', 'Learner Driver' and much more. There are also 'Family Active' holidays for all the family and centres in France. Winter snow sports are available in Austria. Telephone for free brochure. **Check out page 8.**

BOWLING (TEN PIN)

EAST SUSSEX: Bexhill: **Ocean Bowling** Ravenside Retail Pk 01424 730014. Brighton: **Brighton Bowlplex** Brighton Marina 01273 818180. Eastbourne: **Lloyd's Lanes** Broadwater Way Hampden Pk 01323 509999.
WEST SUSSEX: Crawley: **Hollywood Bowl** Ifield Ave 01293 521999. Horsham: **Superbowl** Horsham Pk off Albion Way 01403 274642. Worthing: **AMF Bowling** Marine Pde 01903 230835.

CERAMIC & POTTERY PAINTING

EAST SUSSEX: Brighton: **The Painting Pottery Cafe** 31 North Rd North Laines 01273 628952, **Paint Pots** 39 Trafalgar St 01273 696682. Rye: **Paint Pots** Conduit Hill 01797 222033.
WEST SUSSEX: Bognor Regis: **Glazed Expressions** Aldwick Rd 01243 824917. Chichester: **Ceramica** Midland House 01243 788766. Haywards Heath: **Fun Pots** 16 Sussex Rd 01444 414234.

WEST SUSSEX: Bolney: **Have-A-Go Hobby Pottery Painting,** Unit 1 Cross Post Industrial Park on A272, www.have-a-go.co.uk 01444 882106. A wonderful place to try out pottery painting with friendly, helpful guidance on hand. Choose from a wide selection of items to decorate including ornaments, boxes, vases and Christmas decorations. Use stencils or create your own design, before firing in the kiln for collection later; acrylics can be taken home immediately. Great fun for all ages, even `tinies' will enjoy placing a handprint on a plate. Groups and parties must pre-book and booking recommended during school hols. Open Mon, 1.30-4.30pm, Tues-Thurs, 10am-12noon & 1.30-4.30pm, Sat 10am-1pm. Fri during school hols, 10am-12noon & 1.30-4.30pm. Adults only Tues & Thurs, 7-9pm. Birthdays **Check out page 8.**

CINEMAS

EAST SUSSEX: Bexhill: **Curzon Picture Playhouse** Western Rd 01424 223950. Brighton: **Duke of York's Cinema** Preston Circus 01273 602503, **The Odeon** Kingswest Centre West St 08705 050007, **UGC Cinemas** Marina Village 08701 555145. Eastbourne: **Curzon Cinema** Langney Rd 01323 731441, **UGC Cinemas** Pevensey Bay Rd 08701 555159. Hailsham: **The Pavilion** George St 01323 841414. Hastings: **Odeon** Queens Rd 08705 050007. Uckfield: **The Picture House** High St 01825 763822.
WEST SUSSEX: Bognor Regis: **The Picturedrome** 51 Canada Gro 01243 823138. Burgess Hill: **Orion Cinema** Cyprus Rd 01444 243300. Chichester: **Chichester Cinema** New Park Rd 01243 786650. Crawley: **The Hawth** Hawth Ave 01293 553636, **UGC Cinemas** 0870 9020411. East Grinstead: **The King St Picture House** King St 01342 321666. Haywards Heath: **Clair Hall** Perrymount Rd 01444 455440. Littlehampton: **Windmill Entertainment Centre** The Green 01903 722224. Worthing: **The Connaught Theatre** Union Pl 01903 206206, **Dome Cinema** Marine Pde 01903 823112.

CLIMBING

EAST SUSSEX: Battle: **Area Sports Centre** Claverham Community College 01424 774772. Crowborough: **Evolution Climbing Centre** 01892 862924. Eridge Green: **Bowles Outdoor Centre** 01892 665665. Groombridge: **Soft Rock Climbing** 01892 863659. Lamberhurst: **Bewl Water Outdoor Centre** 01892 890716.

Crowborough: **Evolution Indoor Climbing,** Lye Green, www.evolutionclimbingwall.co.uk 01892 862924, is an indoor rock climbing centre designed for climbers of all abilities. There are over 100 graded bouldering problems, with a separate teaching area, abseil tower, climbing equipment shop and a special training 'Woody' Bouldering Room. Tuition is provided by fully qualified instructors with many years experience. Climbers can progress at their own pace to the outside crags, mix and match between the indoors and outdoors and enjoy an altogether more rewarding climbing experience. Activities are arranged to maximise enjoyment for both individuals and groups. Open daily, till late. Birthdays **Open all year Check out page 10.**

Groombridge, **Soft Rock Climbing** (Harrison's Rocks), just over the border in Kent, www.softrockclimbing.co.uk 01892 863659, provides a rare opportunity for all ages to try climbing under the supervision of fully qualified, experienced instructors, who make the climbing safe, fun and educational. At all times special emphasis is given to promoting safety and good practice. A coaching scheme, holiday courses and personal tuition are offered, plus unique birthday parties where low level climbs, exciting races and fun, are tailored to the individual ability of the children. Access to Evolution Indoor Climbing facility for late evening birthday parties and turn up and climb sessions. All safety equipment is provided and the instructors are registered with the Adventure Activities Licensing Authority. Bookings by arrangement. Schools Birthdays **Open all year.**

CRAZY & ADVENTURE GOLF

EAST SUSSEX: Bexhill: on the seafront at West Parade. Brighton: Seafront. Eastbourne: Princes Park, seafront next to Treasure Island, Fort Fun. Hastings: The Stade on the seafront, White Rock Gardens. Lewes: Salts Rec Ground.
WEST SUSSEX: Birdham: Earnley Gardens. Bognor Regis: Hotham Park. Hunston: Chichester Golf. Littlehampton: Harbour Park, Norfolk Gardens, Western Putting.

GO KARTING

EAST SUSSEX: Eastbourne: **Trax Indoor Karting** Hampden Park Ind Est 01323 521133, **Fort Fun** Royal Pde 01323 642833. Polegate: **Kart Track Ltd** Filching Manor Motor Museum 01323 487933.
WEST SUSSEX: Crawley: **Go Karting For Fun** Gatwick Rd 0870 6000 601.

LANGUAGE COURSES

WEST SUSSEX: Cambridge Language & Activity Courses. CLAC, www.clac.org.uk 01223 240340, organises interesting Summer courses for 8-13 year and 14-17 year olds at two separate sites in lovely countryside locations, Lavant House and Slindon College, West Sussex. The idea is to bring together British and foreign students to create natural language exchange in a motivated and fun environment. There are French, German and Spanish classes for British students and English for overseas students. Fully supervised in a safe environment, there are lots of activities such as swimming, tennis, team games and competitions, drama and music, in addition to the language tuition. Residential or not, these courses offer enjoyable multi-activity weeks with 20 hours of specific tuition in small groups. Courses run weekly during July and August. Please call for more details and a brochure. Birthdays **Check out page 10.**

MUSIC AND MOVEMENT

Jo Jingles, www.jojingles.co.uk 01494 719360, is a leading music and singing experience with an educational slant for children aged 6 months to 7 years. Exciting and stimulating classes run at venues all over the country. For details on classes in your area or for information on the franchise opportunity please call 01494 719360, email: headoffice@jojingles.co.uk or visit the website. Birthdays **Check out page 10.**

Monkey Music, www.monkeymusic.co.uk 01582 766464, runs music classes for babies and children aged between 6 months and 4 years at venues all over the UK. Business franchise opportunities are available in this area. Please telephone for details. **Check out page 16.**

PITCH AND PUTT

EAST SUSSEX: Brighton Area: Roedean, Rottingdean. Hastings: East Hill. Hove: Kingsway. Lewes: The Convent Field. Seaford: Salt's Rec Ground.
WEST SUSSEX: Crawley: Goffs Park. Haywards Heath: Beech Hurst Gdns. Hunston: Chichester Golf. Littlehampton: Norfolk Gdns. Warnham: Rookwood Golf Course. Worthing: Brooklands Park.

PUTTING GREENS

EAST SUSSEX: Bexhill: Egerton Pk, The Metropole Lawns West Pde. Eastbourne: Princes Pk, Helen Gdns. Hastings: The Stade on the seafront. Rye: Town Salts. Seaford: Salts Rec Ground. St. Leonards-on-Sea: West Marina.
WEST SUSSEX: Arundel: Mill Rd. Bognor Regis: Blakes Rd Felpham, Hotham Park, Marine Pk Gdns. Chichester: Oaklands Park. Crawley: Goffs Park, Langley Green playing field. East

Grinstead: Mount Noddy. Haywards Heath: Beech Hurst Gdns. Littlehampton: Maltravers Pk, Western Putting. Worthing: Brooklands Park,

Sports & Leisure

QUAD BIKING

WEST SUSSEX: East Grinstead: **Leisure Pursuits** 01342 825522. Check out `Trips' chapter. Hurstpierpoint: **Quadland** Washbrooks Farm (Pre-booked only) 01273 834403.

ROLLER SKATING, BOARDING & BMX

EAST SUSSEX: Brighton: The Level BMX SB, Preston Park RS. Crowborough: Jarvis Brook SB. Eastbourne: Cross Levels Way BMX, Sovereign Park BMX RS SB, Shinewater SB. Hastings: Salaise Rd BMX RS SB. Pevensey: Walls End Rd Pevensey Bay BMX. Seaford: Chalvington Field RS SB, Salt's Rec Ground RS. Uckfield: Victoria Pleasure Ground SB.
WEST SUSSEX: Aldwick: Avisford Park RS SB. Arundel: Canada Rd RS SB. Bognor Regis: Esplanade Gdns RS SB. Bolney: Rec Ground RS. Burgess Hill: St John's Park BMX RS SB. Chichester: Westgate Leisure Centre BMX RS SB. Crawley: Crawley Leisure Centre BMX RS SB. East Grinstead: East Court College La BMX RS SB, Kings LC BMX RS SB. East Wittering: Rec Ground BMX RS SB. Haywards Heath: Victoria Park BMX RS SB. Horsham: Horsham Park BMX RS SB. Littlehampton: Eldon Way BMX, Linden Rec Ground RS SB, Sea Rd RS SB. Midhurst: Rec Ground BMX RS SB. Partridge Green: Rec Ground RS SB. Roffey: Southomes Rec Ground RS SB. Rudgwick: Rec Ground RS SB. Selsey: East Beach Amenity Area BMX RS SB. Southwater: Easteds Meadow BMX. Southwick: Rec Ground SB. Steyning: Rec Ground RS SB. Upper Beeding: Rec Ground BMX RS SB. West Chiltington: Rec Ground RS SB. Worthing: Homefield Park BMX RS SB.

SKIING AND SNOWBOARDING

EAST SUSSEX: Eridge Green: **Bowles Outdoor Centre** 01892 665665.

Hailsham: **Knockhatch Ski Centre,** www.knockhatch.com 01323 843344. Enjoy skiing and snowboarding on the nursery and 110 metre slopes, and visit the new Edge to Edge ski and board shop for equipment rental and clothing. Lessons and birthday parties can be booked. **Check out Knockhatch Adventure Park in 'Adventure' chapter and page 40.**

SPORTS AND LEISURE CENTRES

Abbreviations: RC: Recreation Centre, SC: Sports Centre, SH: Sports Hall.
* Centre has a swimming pool.

EAST SUSSEX: Bexhill: **Bexhill LC** Down Rd 01424 731171. Brighton: **Moulsecoomb Community LC** Moulsecoomb Way 01273 622266, **Stanley Deason LC** Wilson Ave 01273 694281, **Withdean SC** Tongdean La 01273 542100. Crowborough: **Goldsmiths LC** Eridge Rd 01892 665488. Eastbourne: **Cavendish SC** Eldon Rd 01323 647683, **Hampden Park SC** Brodrick Rd 01323 509859. Hailsham: **Lagoon LC*** Vicarage La 01323 846755. Hastings: **Summerfields LC*** Bohemia Rd 01424 781777. Heathfield: **Heathfield LC** Cade St Old Heathfield 01435 868824. Hove: **King Alfred LC*** Kingsway 01273 290290. Lewes: **Lewes LC*** Mountfield Rd 01273 486000. Peacehaven: **Meridian LC** Greenwich Way 01273 588858. Portslade: **Portslade SC** Chalky Rd 01273 411100. Seaford: **Downs LC** Sutton Rd 01323 490011. Shinewater: **Shinewater SC** Milfoil Dr Langney 01323 768614. Uckfield: **Utopia LC** Downsview Cresc 01825 761722.
WEST SUSSEX: Bognor Regis: **Arun LC*** Felpham Way 01243 826612. Burgess Hill: **The Triangle LC*** Triangle Way 01444 876000. Chichester: **Westgate LC*** Via Ravenna 01243 785651. Crawley: **Bewbush LC** Breezehurst Dr 01293 546477, **Crawley LC*** Haslett Ave 01293 537431. East Grinstead: **Kings LC*** Moat Rd 01342 328616. Haywards Heath: **Dolphin LC***

13

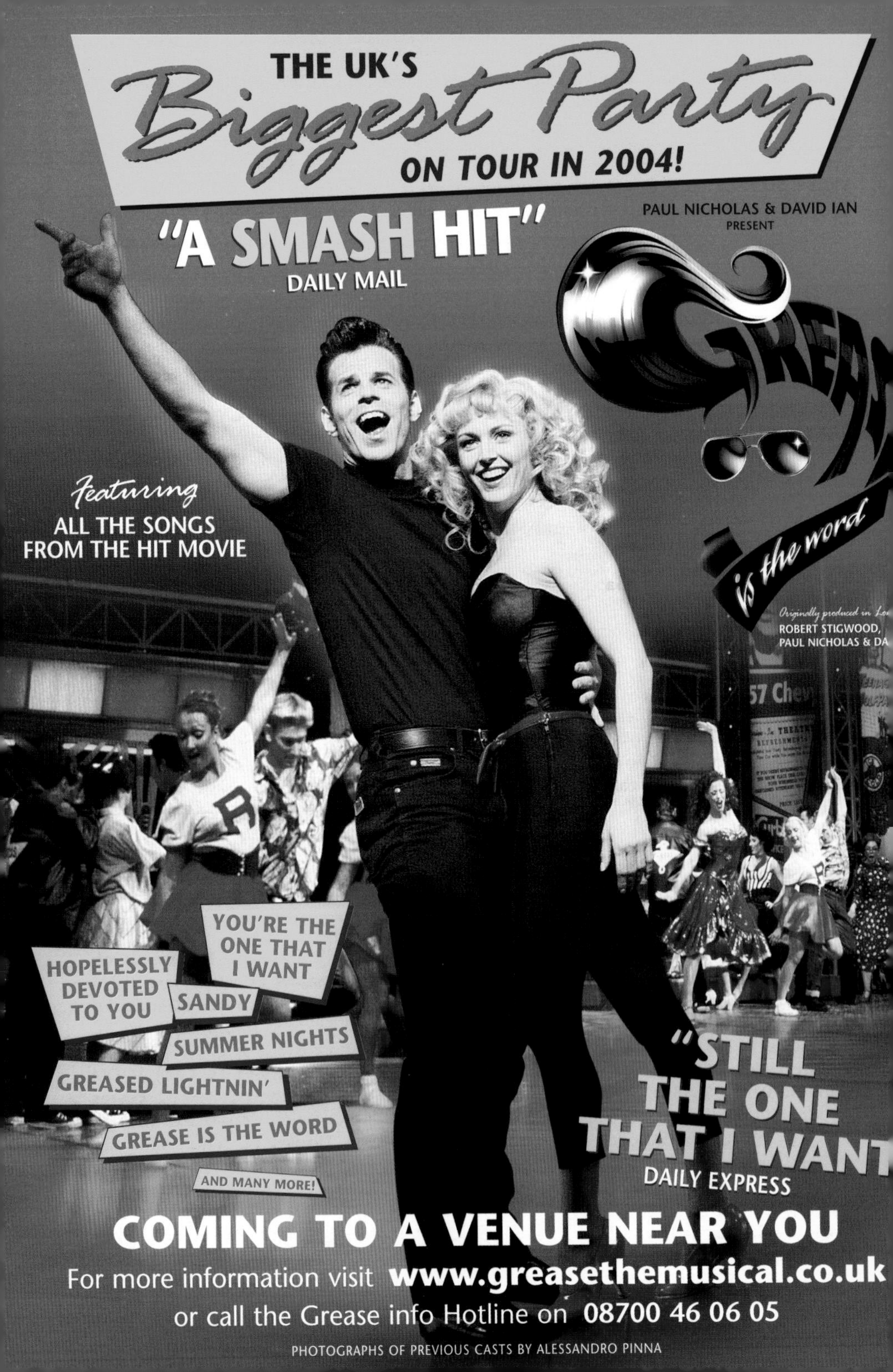

THE UK'S **Biggest Party** ON TOUR IN 2004!

"A SMASH HIT"
DAILY MAIL

PAUL NICHOLAS & DAVID IAN
PRESENT

Featuring
ALL THE SONGS
FROM THE HIT MOVIE

GREASE
is the word

Originally produced in Lo...
ROBERT STIGWOOD,
PAUL NICHOLAS & DA...

YOU'RE THE ONE THAT I WANT

HOPELESSLY DEVOTED TO YOU SANDY

SUMMER NIGHTS

GREASED LIGHTNIN'

GREASE IS THE WORD

AND MANY MORE!

"STILL THE ONE THAT I WANT
DAILY EXPRESS

COMING TO A VENUE NEAR YOU
For more information visit **www.greasethemusical.co.uk**
or call the Grease info Hotline on 08700 46 06 05

PHOTOGRAPHS OF PREVIOUS CASTS BY ALESSANDRO PINNA

Pasture Hill Rd 01444 457337. Henfield: **Henfield LC** The Kingsfield 01273 494984. Horsham: **Broadbridge Heath LC** Wickhurst La 01403 211311, **The Pavilions in the Park** Hurst Road 01403 219200. Lancing: **Lancing Manor LC** Old Shoreham Rd 01273 263300. Littlehampton: **Swimming and SC*** Sea Rd 01903 725451. Midhurst: **The Grange LC** Bepton Rd 01730 816841. Southwater: **Southwater LC** Pevensey Rd 01403 733208. Southwick: **Southwick LC** Old Barn Way off Manor Hall Rd 01273 263200. Steyning: **Steyning LC*** Horsham Rd 01903 879666. Storrington: **Chanctonbury LC** Spierbridge Rd 01903 746070. Westergate: **Six Villages SC** Lime Ave 01243 546830. Worthing: **Worthing LC** Shaftesbury Ave 01903 502237, **Davison LC** Selborne Rd 01903 204668.

SWIMMING POOLS (INDOOR)

Check out `Sports & Leisure Centres' listing above. Those marked with an * have a pool.

EAST SUSSEX: Brighton: **Prince Regent Swimming Complex** Church St 01273 685692. Eastbourne: **Motcombe Pool** Motcombe Rd 01323 410748, **Sovereign Centre** Royal Pde 01323 738822. Newhaven: **Seahaven Pool** Chapel St 01273 512498. Seaford: **Seaford Head Swimming Pool** Arundel Rd. 01323 897632.
WEST SUSSEX: Shoreham: **Wadurs Community Pool** Kingston Broadway 01273 263100. Worthing: **Aquarena** Brighton Rd 01903 231797.

SWIMMING POOLS (OUTDOOR)

EAST SUSSEX: Brighton: **Saltdean Lido** 01273 880616. Lewes: **The Pels Swimming Pool** 01273 472334.
WEST SUSSEX: Burgess Hill: **Triangle Leisure Centre** 01444 876000.

THEATRES

Grease on Tour, www.greasethemusical.co.uk Grease the Musical is on tour throughout the country this year and is going to be at a theatre near you! The show is packed with explosive energy, vibrant 1950s pop culture and lots of unforgettable songs. Take the family to this fabulous Rock'n'Roll musical filled with irresistible groovy and memorable moments. Don't miss it! For full information, casting details, competitions, special offers and full tour venues and dates log on to the website above. **Check out page 14.**

EAST SUSSEX: Bexhill-on-Sea: **De La Warr Pavilion** Marina 01424 787949. Brighton: **Brighton Centre** Kings Rd 01273 290131, **Brighton Dome** New Rd 01273 709709, **Gardner Arts Centre** University of Sussex 01273 685861, **New Venture Theatre** Bedford Pl 01273 746118, **Sallis Benney Theatre** University of Brighton 01273 643010, **Theatre Royal** New Rd 01273 328488. Eastbourne: **The Congress Theatre** Carlisle Rd, **Devonshire Park Theatre** Compton St, **Royal Hippodrome** Seaside Rd, **Winter Gardens** Carlisle Rd, all bookings and enquiries 01323 412000. Hastings: **Phoenix Arts Centre** Parkstone Rd 01424 722612, **Stables Theatre** The Bourne 01424 423221, **White Rock Theatre** seafront 01424 781000.
WEST SUSSEX: Arundel: **The Priory Playhouse** London Rd 01903 883345. Bognor Regis: **The Alexandra Theatre Arts & Exhibition Centre** Belmont St 01243 862020. Burgess Hill: **Martlets Hall** Martlets Shopping Centre 01444 242888. Crawley: **The Hawth** Hawth Ave 01293 553636, **Ifield Barn Theatre** Rectory La 01293 525030. Chichester: **Chichester Festival Theatre & Minerva Theatre** Oaklands Pk 01243 781312. East Grinstead: **Chequer Mead Theatre & Arts Centre** De La Warr Rd 01342 302000. Glyndebourne: **Glyndebourne Festival Opera** 01273 812321. Goring by Sea: **The Northbrook Theatre** Littlehampton Rd 01903 606162. Haywards Heath: **Clair Hall** Perrymount Rd 01444 455440. Horsham: **Christs Hospital Theatre** Christs Hospital 01403 247434. Littlehampton: **Windmill Entertainment Centre** The Green 01903 722224. Worthing: **The Connaught Theatre**

Union Pl, **Pavilion Theatre** Marine Pde, **Assembly Hall** Stoke Abbott Rd, all bookings and enquiries 01903 206206.

WATERSPORTS

EAST SUSSEX: Eastbourne: **Spray Watersports** opp. Princes Pk 01323 417023 K S W. Eridge Green: **Bowles Outdoor Centre** 01892 665665 C. Hove: **Lagoon Watersports** 01273 424842 PB RB S W. Lamberhurst: **Bewl Water Outdoor Centre** 01892 890716 C K S, **Bewl Windsurfing** 01892 891000 W. Seaford: **Seven Sisters Country Pk** 01323 491289 C K RB.

WEST SUSSEX: Ardingly: **Activity Centre** 01444 892549 C K RB S W. Bosham: **Bosham Sailing** Bosham La 01243 572555 S. Crawley: **Tilgate Lake** 01293 419351 C K S. East Grinstead: **Kings Leisure Centre** Moat Rd 01342 328616 C. Horsham: **Southwater Watersports Centre** 01403 734424 C K RB S W.

YOUTH HOSTELLING

Introduce children to Youth Hostels for years of enjoyable family holidays! There are over 200 Youth Hostels in England and Wales based in towns, cities, on the coast or in the countryside and most have family rooms. You can self-cater or be cooked for, stay for one night or as long as you like; youth hostelling offers flexibility and choice. New for 2004 is the 'Top Bunk Club', especially for children aged 5-12 years. To find out more visit www.yha.org.uk or call 0870 770 8868 and quote 'Let's Go 04'. For details of 25% off membership offer **check out below.**

History, Art & Science

Step back in time and find out about the past, explore the world of art and design or discover the mysteries of the universe, science and technology. The places listed here have admission charges, but there are many wonderful museums and places of interest, which are free to visit. Check out the `Free Places' chapter.

EAST SUSSEX

Battle, Battle Abbey, EH, 01424 773792. A visit here gives an insight into one of the best known events in English history, the Battle of Hastings, 1066. Although much has been ruined, the gatehouse still dominates the town and other parts of the original buildings remain. Special events take place throughout the year. Museum. Telephone for opening times and prices. Schools **Open all year.**

Buckley's Yesterday's World, 90 High Street, www.yesterdaysworld.co.uk 01424 774269, is a fascinating arcade of shops, crammed with thousands of delightful exhibits from days past. Play the old fashioned slot machines and enjoy the miniature fairground and children's play area. Open daily, 10am, closing times vary. Schools **Open all year** Price B.

Bexhill, Bexhill Costume Museum, Manor Gardens, Upper Sea Road, 01424 210045, contains a fascinating collection of costumes from the mid 18th century, set amongst children's toys and dolls and a variety of household items. Open daily, Apr-Oct, 10.30am-4.30pm, Sat and Sun, 2-4.30pm. Closed Weds in Apr, May & Oct, but subject to change. Schools Price A.

Bexhill Museum, Egerton Road, www.bexhill-museum.co.uk 01424 787950, covers archaeology, local and natural histories as well as cultures of other lands. Unusual displays include the cast of a dinosaur footprint and remains of a woolly mammoth and woolly rhinoceros! Questionnaires and holiday activities. Open Feb-Dec, Tues-Fri, 10am-5pm, weekends and Bank Hol Mons, 2-5pm. Schools Price A.

Brighton, Preston Manor, Preston Park, 01273 292770, is an Edwardian house, set in lovely grounds. As well as the beautifully furnished rooms, there are servants' quarters and a restored kitchen. Schools can take a trip back in time with role-play. Open Tues-Sat and Bank Hols, 10am-5pm, Sun, 2-5pm, Mon, 1-5pm. Schools **Open all year** Price A.

The Royal Pavilion, www.royalpavilion.org.uk 01273 290900, England's Taj Mahal, is a magnificent building in Indian style, completed in 1822. The interior is exotically furnished in Chinese taste. Special events throughout the year. Open daily, Oct-Mar, 10.30am-5.15pm, Apr-Sept, 9.30am-5.45pm. Schools **Open all year** Price B.

Toy and Model Museum, 52-55 Trafalgar Street, www.brightontoymuseum.co.uk 01273 749494, contains three working model railway layouts and a large collection of toys from the last century as well as some even older than that. Open Tues-Fri, 10am-5pm, Sat, 11am-5pm. Schools **Open all year** Price A.

Burwash, Bateman's, NT, 01435 882302, was the home of Rudyard Kipling and contains many momentos from his stories including illustrations of Mowgli, Baloo and Shere Khan from the Jungle Book. Working water mill, wild garden, tearoom and shop open Mar, Sat & Sun. House open 3rd Apr-31st Oct, Sat-Wed and Good Fri, 11am-5pm. Schools Price B.

Ditchling, Ditchling Museum, Church Lane, www.ditchling-museum.com 01273 844744, is housed in the Victorian school and tells the story of the village and its people. Excellent questionnaires will encourage children to hunt for items both everyday and unusual - find out what sort of creature is a Wyvern! `Loan boxes' available for schools. Open mid Feb-mid Dec, Tues-Sat & Bank Hol Mons, 10.30am-5pm, Sun 2-5pm. Schools Price A.

Eastbourne, Heritage Centre, 2 Carlisle Road, 01323 411189, looks at the history of Eastbourne and includes a video. Open Easter-Sept, Sun-Fri and Bank Hols, 2-5pm. Groups by appointment all year. Schools Price A.

How We Lived Then, 20 Cornfield Terrace, 01323 737143, is a museum of shops and social history. Browse through the authentic Victorian-style shops and find everything from sweets to musical instruments and toys. Open daily, 10am-5.30pm. Schools **Open all year** Price B.

Redoubt Fortress Museum, Royal Parade, www.eastbournemuseums.co.uk 01323 410300, is housed in the impressive circular, moated fortress. Groups can have hands-on sessions with original objects. There are also musket firing demonstrations as well as special events in May/Jun for `Museums Month'. Open daily, 1st Apr-5th Nov, 9.30am-5.30pm. Schools Price B.

Wish Tower Puppet Museum, Martello Tower, www.puppets.co.uk 01323 417776. Fascinating displays including early television puppets like Muffin the Mule, and Punch and Judy puppets from around the world. Some puppets are available for hands-on activities. Open Sat-Sun only, Easter-Sept, 11am-5pm, daily in Summer hols. Schools Price A.

Hailsham, Michelham Priory, Upper Dicker, 01323 844224. A Sussex Past property. A medieval moat, nearly a mile long, tests the most energetic of young legs and enclosed within it is part of a beautiful Augustinian priory incorporated into a splendid Tudor mansion. Inside, there is a fascinating array of exhibits and outside the picturesque gardens are enhanced by a 14th century gatehouse, working watermill, physic herb and cloister gardens, smithy, rope museum, old farm wagons and a dramatic Elizabethan Great Barn. Across the moat there is a large picnic and play area. The education department provides a full service to schools and there are also holiday activities and a number of special event days for families including an Easter Garden Festival, May Day Festival and Halloween event. Open Mar-Oct, Tues-Sun & Bank Hol Mons, (daily in Aug); Mar & Oct, 10.30am-4pm; Apr-Jul & Sept, 10.30am-5pm; Aug, 10.30am-5.30pm. Schools Price B.

Halland, Bentley Wildfowl and Motor Museum. The motor museum houses a collection of superb veteran, Edwardian and vintage cars and motorcycles. Check out 'Farms' chapter. Schools Birthdays Price B.

Hastings, Hastings Castle, www.hastings.gov.uk 01424 781112, is now a ruin with parts of the walls and gatehouse remaining but there are mysterious whispering dungeons and superb views. The `1066 Story' is well told. Open daily, mid Feb-Mar, Oct-Nov, 11am-4pm; Sept-Oct, Apr-Jul, 10am-5pm, Aug, 10am-5.30pm, Dec-mid Feb, 11am-3.30pm. Schools **Open all year** Price A.

Smugglers Adventure, in St. Clements Cave, West Hill, www.discoverhastings.co.uk 01424 422964, is an exciting story of smuggling in the 18th century brought to life by dramatic effects and wax models. Explore the underground passages with `Hairy Jack' and watch out for the dangers experienced by the men of old. Open daily, Summer, 10am-5.30pm, Winter, 11am-4.30pm. Schools **Open all year** Price B.

Herstmonceux, The Observatory Science Centre, www.theobservatory.org 01323 832731. Housed in the former home of the Royal Greenwich Observatory, this exciting hands-on science centre offers the opportunity to have great fun with different scientific concepts using over 100 interactive exhibits. Enjoy regular tours of the historic telescopes and domes. The outdoor Discovery Park has large-scale exhibits including energy track, balance boards, magic sticks, echo tubes and more. An excellent programme of special events and children's activities includes different themed Science Experience days. Open 10th Jan-12th Dec, times vary. Schools Birthdays Price B **Check out page 22.**

Hove, The British Engineerium, Nevill Road, www.britishengineerium.com 01273 559583. Housed within a beautifully restored Victorian pumping station, there are hundreds of model as well as full size steam engines, an interactive exhibition and more. Boilers are alight and engines in steam on the first Sunday in the month. Open daily, 10am-5pm. Schools **Open all year** Price B.

Lewes, Anne of Cleves House, 52 Southover High St, 01273 474610. A Sussex Past property. This house formed part of Anne's divorce settlement from Henry VIII in 1541. The 16th century timber-framed Wealden hall-house contains wide-ranging collections of Sussex interest. Furnished rooms give an impression of life in the 17th and 18th centuries. Exhibits include artefacts from nearby Lewes Priory, Sussex pottery and Wealden ironwork. The house and museum provide a superb focus for Tudor studies and in addition to school parties, the education department arranges a varied programme of holiday activities. Open Mar-Oct, Tues-Sat, 10am-5pm, Sun, Mon & Bank Hols, 11am-5pm; Nov-Feb, Tues-Sat, 10am-5pm. Schools **Open all year** Price A.

Lewes Castle, Barbican House, 169 High Street, 01273 486290. A Sussex Past property. The distinctive octagonal towers of Lewes' imposing Norman Castle provide an invigorating climb rewarded by magnificent views of the county town and surrounding downland countryside. Across the road, spanned by the towering Barbican Gate, is Barbican House where fascinating displays follow the progress of Sussex people from their earliest beginnings. The `Story of Lewes Town' draws children of all ages. It is a superb scale model of Victorian Lewes providing the centrepiece of an engrossing 25-minute audio-visual show; a touch-screen computer provides further insight. The education department offers a wide range of facilities for school groups as well as numerous holiday activities. Open Tues-Sat, 10am-5.30pm, Mon, Suns & Bank Hols, 11am-5.30pm. Closes at dusk in Winter and Mons in Jan. Schools **Open all year** Price B.

Lewes(near), Firle Place, 01273 858307, is a beautiful house full of wonderful pictures and porcelain, in a lovely setting. The detailed guided tours are more suitable for older children. Open Jun-Sept, Sun, Wed & Thurs, 2-4.30pm. Also Bank Hol Suns and Mons, Easter-Aug. Restaurant open 12noon-4.30pm. Price B.

Newhaven, Newhaven Fort, www.newhavenfort.org.uk 01273 517622. Step into wartime Britain at this 10-acre coastal fortress. Journey from Napoleon to World War II through a maze of exciting exhibitions, underground tunnels and clifftop ramparts. There is a children's special mission trail. Play area for under 12s. Open daily, Mar-Oct and weekends in Nov, 10.30am-6pm. Schools Price B.

Pevensey, Pevensey Castle, EH, 01323 762604, is a Norman castle, now in ruins, enclosed within a Roman fort. Look out for the prisons! Events are staged here in season. Tearooms. Open daily. Telephone for opening times and prices. Schools **Open all year.**

Polegate, Filching Manor Motor Museum, Jevington Road, Wannock, 01323 487838, houses some of the world's rarest sports and racing cars, specialist model cars, equipment and motoring memorabilia. There is also a 600m karting track for adults and older children all year. Karting and entry to museum is by appointment only. Open Easter-Oct, Sun and Bank Hol Mons. Tours at 11am and 2.30pm. Schools Price B.

Polegate Windmill and Milling Museum, Park Croft, 01323 734496. This tower mill has been restored and the museum displays milling bygones. Open Sun and Bank Hols, Easter-Oct, 2-5pm. Also Weds in Aug for special children's events. For group bookings telephone 01323 644727. Schools Price A.

Portslade, Foredown Tower, Foredown Road, 01273 292092, is a nature and astronomy centre with a camera obscura at the top which gives a unique bird's eye view of the surrounding area. Demonstrations are given hourly and regular events held during school hols. Telephone for opening times. Schools Price A.

Robertsbridge, Bodiam Castle, NT, 01580 830436, is an impressive fairytale castle. Although much of the interior is in ruins, a moat surrounds the outside walls and children will love to climb the spiral stairs within the remaining towers and explore the battlements. Quiz available. Special events. Open daily, 14th Feb-31st Oct, 10am-6pm (or dusk, if earlier), 1st Nov-13th Feb, Sat-Sun only, 10am-4pm (or dusk, if earlier). Schools Birthdays **Open all year** Price B.

Rye, Heritage Centre & Rye Town Model, Strand Quay, www.ryeheritage.co.uk 01797 226696, is the place to learn about this historic town. Watch out for smugglers as many fascinating tales are told with excellent light and sound effects (not recommended for children under 4). Ghost tour and town walk audio tapes may be hired. Gift shop and Information Centre. Open daily, Mar-Oct, 9.30am-5pm (Suns, 10am-5pm), Nov-Feb, 10am-4pm. Schools **Open all year** Price A.

Rye Castle and Museum, Gun Garden, 01797 226728. Housed at two sites, the Ypres Tower and No. 3 East Street, this collection includes local wartime memorabilia, toys, costumes and an old fire engine built in 1745. Open Thurs-Mon, Apr-Oct, 10.30am-1pm, 2-5pm. Ypres Tower only, Nov-Mar, Sat & Sun, 10.30am-1pm, 2-3.30pm. Schools **Open all year** Price A.

TRAVEL GAMES

What can you see from the car window?
If there are 2 or more of you, who can see the following things first?
Keep score!

Caravan	Zebra crossing	Traffic lights
Dog	Black and white cows	Bridge
Motorway sign	Car transporter	Milk float
Tunnel	Sheep	Stretch limousine
Level crossing	Red letter box	Telephone box

WEST SUSSEX

Amberley, Amberley Working Museum, www.amberleymuseum.co.uk 01798 831370, is a busy, working museum set in a former quarry. Observe different crafts, ride on a workman's train or vintage open top bus and enjoy the nature trail. Informative exhibitions include BT, road making, electricity and radio. Open mid Mar-end Oct, 10am-5.30pm, Wed-Sun and Bank Hol Mons. Open daily in school hols during that period. Restaurant. Schools Price B.

Arundel, Arundel Castle, www.arundelcastle.org 01903 883136, both enchanting and exciting, is set in magnificent grounds. High on a hill, it is both an ancient castle and a stately home. Outside, climb to the top of the Norman motte and keep, and marvel at the grand interior and impressive armoury on display inside. Restaurant and shop. Open Apr-Oct, Sun-Fri, 12noon-5pm. Schools Price C.

Arundel Museum and Heritage Centre, 61 High St, 01903 885708 recounts the history of Arundel in interesting displays, models and photographs. Quizzes and activities available at all time. Open Apr-Sept, Mon-Sat, 10am-5pm, Sun, 2-5pm. Schools Price A.

Bignor, Bignor Roman Villa, www.pyrrha.demon.co.uk 01798 869259, set in superb countryside, is well worth visiting to see some fine mosaics including Medusa in the bath-house changing room, Venus and Cupid gladiators, Ganymede and Eagle. All the mosaics are in their original location and under cover. Walk on genuine Roman floors, see the hypocaust system and learn how it worked. Hands-on opportunities for spinning wool, making mosaics and writing on wax tablets at weekends and during school hols. Additional activities available for school visits. Open Mar-Apr, Tues-Sun & Bank Hols; May-Oct, daily, 10am-5pm, (6pm, Jun-Sept). Schools Price B **Check out page 22.**

Chichester, Fishbourne Roman Palace, Salthill Road, Fishbourne, 01243 785859. A Sussex Past property. Initially a military supply base established at the time of the Roman invasion in AD43, the sumptuous palace itself was constructed around AD75. Visitors can see many of the remains including twenty spectacular mosaic floors. The superb Roman garden has been replanted to its original plan and a Roman gardening museum displays a range of replica horticultural tools and equipment as well as original implements found on the site. The story of Fishbourne is told in the main museum and by an audio-visual programme. Thousands of school children study the Romans here every year, where there are purpose-built educational facilities. Open daily, Feb & Nov-15th Dec, 10am-4pm; Mar-Jul & Sept-Oct, 10am-5pm; Aug, 10am-6pm; Jan & 16th-31st Dec, Sat & Sun only, 10am-4pm. Schools **Open all year** Price B.

Mechanical Music and Doll Collection, Church Road, Portfield, 01243 372646, is housed in a Victorian church which provides a special atmosphere to view the collection of dolls and hear the music-making machines play. Open Jun-Sept, Wed, 1-4pm. Group visits outside normal hours can be arranged. Schools Price A.

South Downs Planetarium and Science Centre, situated at the southern end of the Chichester High Schools Campus, off Kingsham Road, 01243 774400. This planetarium offers the chance to explore the excitement of the universe through presentations in the star theatre, lasting 50-60 mins. Not suitable for under 7s. Telephone for presentation times. Schools Price B.

East Grinstead, Hammerwood Park, www.hammerwoodpark.com 01342 850594, off the
A264, built in the Greek revival style, is of particular interest to those studying the classics, especially Ancient Greece. Young musicians are encouraged to play the pianos and splendid pipe organ. Open Jun-Sept, Wed, Sat and Bank Hol Mons, 2-5pm. Group visits by arrangement. Schools Price B.

Standen, NT, 01342 323029, is an 1890s house of interest to older children. The beautiful interior is full of William Morris designs. There is a lovely woodland walk and picnic area. A quiz is available as well as holiday and weekend activities. Open 27th Mar-31st Oct, Wed-Sun, Bank Hol Mons, 11am-5pm, 5th Nov-19th Dec, Fri-Sun, 11am-3pm. Schools Price B.

Gatwick Airport, Skyview, 4th Floor, South Terminal, 01293 502244. Gain an insight into
a day in the life of Gatwick, enjoy a multi-media show and go on a tour of an historic airliner as well as the nose cone of a Comet Jet. Experience the thrills of a simulator ride! Open daily, 7am-7pm, (Winter 9am-4pm). Schools **Open all year** Price A.

Goodwood, Goodwood House, www.goodwood.co.uk 01243 755040, on the Goodwood
Estate, home to the Festival of Speed, has fine collections of furniture and paintings. Regular guided tours are held. Open Mar-Oct, 1-5pm, but closes occasionally due to special events. For group bookings telephone 01243 755048. Tearoom. Schools Price B.

Petworth, Petworth Cottage Museum, 346 High Street, 01798 342100, is a chance to see
a 17th century worker's cottage restored as it might have been in 1910. The cottage is well equipped, with gas lights and copies of 1911 daily papers! Open Apr-Oct, Wed-Sun and Bank Hols, 2-4.30pm. Schools Price A.

Petworth House, NT, 01798 342207, is set in a beautiful Deer Park. The house contains an interesting art and sculpture hall. Children's guide and quiz available. Open 27th Mar-31st Oct, Sat-Wed & Good Fri, 11am-5.30pm. Gardens, tearoom and shop. Park open daily, all year until dusk, but closes for concerts. Schools Price B.

Pulborough, Parham, www.parhaminsussex.co.uk 01903 742021, off the A283, is a lovely
Elizabethan manor house with a collection of beautiful furniture, paintings and textiles. The delightful 4-acre walled garden contains a stone built Wendy house and a brick and turf maze as well as a wonderful collection of plants. Restaurant. Open mid Apr-Sept, Wed, Thurs, Sun and Bank Hol Mons, Tues and Fri in Aug. Gardens; 12noon-6pm, House; 2-5pm. Schools Price B.

Rowlands Castle(near), Stansted Park, www.stanstedpark.co.uk 02392 412265, began
as a hunting lodge in the 11th century. The House has an extensive `below stairs' area and purpose built Servants Quarters, giving a wonderful insight into the Edwardian era. Open Apr-Sept, Sun-Mon, Jul-Aug, Sun-Wed, 1-5pm. Grounds open daily. Schools Price B.

Shoreham-by-Sea, Marlipins Museum, High Street, 01273 462994. A Sussex Past
property. Shoreham's local and in particular its maritime history are explored at Marlipins, itself

an important historic Norman building believed to have once been used as a Customs House. The maritime gallery contains many superb models and fine paintings, while the rest of the museum houses exhibits dating back to man's earliest occupation of the area. The development of Shoreham's airport and life in the town during the war years, feature prominently in the displays. Open May-Sept, Tues-Sat, 10.30am-4.30pm. Schools Price A.

Singleton, Weald and Downland Open Air Museum, www.wealddown.co.uk 01243 811348, offers a fascinating day out. Discover 500 years of architectural heritage, enjoy the beautiful parkland setting, visit the farmyard animals and explore over 45 historic buildings. Open daily, Mar-Oct, 10.30am-6pm, Nov-Feb, Sat and Sun, 10.30am-4pm. Schools **Open all year** Price B.

South Harting, Uppark, NT, 01730 825415,is a fine 17th century house situated high on the South Downs. Open daily, 28th Mar-28th Oct, Sun-Thurs, 1-5pm. Grounds, exhibition, shop and restaurant open at 11am-5.30pm. Schools Price B.

Tangmere, Tangmere Military Aviation Museum, www.tangmere-museum.org.uk 01243 775223, tells the story of military flying with aircraft, models, photographs and working displays. Open daily, Feb-Mar and Nov, 10am-4.30pm, Apr-Oct, 10am-5.30pm. Schools Price B.

West Hoathly, The Priest House, North Lane, 01342 810479. A Sussex Past property, standing in the beautiful surroundings of a traditional cottage garden on the edge of Ashdown Forest. The Priest House is an early 15th century timber-framed hall-house. In Elizabethan times it was modernised into a substantial Yeomen's dwelling and is now a folk museum containing country furniture, kitchen equipment, needlework and household items. Outside there is a formal herb garden and the property is a popular destination for local schools studying Tudor times and village life. Open Mar-Oct, Tues-Sat (daily in Aug) and Bank Hol Mons, 10.30am-5.30pm, Sun, 12-5.30pm. Schools Price A.

22

Free Places

Included here are free places of interest in the area, including museums, parks, open spaces, beaches and other places that freely offer family entertainment as well as some ideas of activities you can participate in for free. Although all have free admission, there may be significant car parking charges, extra charges for schools and special activities, or requests for donations. Some of your days out to free places will be the most memorable, if you plan ahead, take a picnic where appropriate and introduce your children to the multitude of free pleasures locally.

EAST SUSSEX

Bexhill, Broadoak Park. Open space for walks, an assault course and the adjacent recreation ground has a play area, tennis courts and football pitches. **Open all year.**

Egerton Park, near the seafront. Lots for children here with an enclosed play park, boating lake, table tennis, tennis courts, putting greens and volleyball. **Open all year.**

Brighton, Booth Museum of Natural History, 194 Dyke Road, www.royalpavilion.org.uk 01273 292777, houses exhibits including birds, butterflies, skeletons, dinosaur bones, fossils and more. Children will enjoy the hands-on discovery gallery. Holiday activities. Open Mon-Wed, Fri-Sat, 10am-5pm, Sun, 2-5pm. Schools **Open all year.**

Brighton Fishing Museum, Arch 201, Brighton seafront, 01273 723064, is in the heart of the fishing quarter where fishermen still mend their nets and sell fish. There are videos and a slide show but the centrepiece is a full size traditional Sussex fishing boat. Open daily, 10am-4pm. Schools **Open all year.**

Brighton Marina, 01273 693636, is the largest yacht marina in Britain and the attractive village square with shops, waterfront pubs and restaurants has a unique atmosphere. **Open all year.**

Brighton Museum and Art Gallery, Church Street, 01273 290900, has a large variety of exhibits which include the body and performance galleries and new children's gallery. Enjoy the interactive displays throughout. Open Tues, 10am-7pm, Wed-Sat, 10am-5pm, Sun 2-5pm. Schools **Open all year.**

Brighton Pier, Madeira Drive, 01273 609361. Traditional pier amusements with kiosks, machines and some very scary funfair rides. Information boards explain the history of the pier. **Open all year.**

The Level, is a small green area to the NE of the town centre, linking the main London and Lewes roads. Edged by a double avenue of elm trees it contains a children's playground, cafe, paddling pool, skateboard run and BMX track. **Open all year.**

Preston Park, has gardens, tennis courts, play area, bowls and cycle track. **Open all year.**

West Pier Play Area is situated 200m W of the West Pier on the seafront. This enclosed play area is lovely for little ones, with sandpits, swings, slides, climbing frames, rope bridges and a paddling pool in the Summer. **Open all year.**

Eastbourne, Gildredge Park, is an attractive wooded area with tennis and basketball courts and children's playground. **Open all year.**

Hampden Park, Lots of open space, tennis courts, a lake and well-equipped children's playground. Eastbourne Sports Park alongside is home to an all-weather athletics track and floodlit football pitch. **Open all year.**

Local History Museum and Towner Art Gallery, High Street, 01323 411688. The museum shows local history from prehistoric times. Charge for special exhibitions. The Art Gallery holds a collection of over 3000 works. Open Tues-Sat, 12noon-5pm, Suns and Bank Hol Mons, 2-5pm. Closed Good Fri. Schools **Open all year.**

The Pier, 01323 410466, is Victorian with many amusements and shops and a newly restored camera obscura. Open 10am-6pm. **Open all year.**

Princes Park, has a large boating lake with pedalos for hire and is a good place for sailing model boats. There is a lakeside cafeteria, mini-golf course, two children's playgrounds and a paddling pool for the under 5s during May-Sept. **Open all year.**

RNLI Museum, Grand Parade, 01323 730717, displays models and pictures of the history of lifeboats. Open daily, Easter-Dec, 10am-5pm (4pm Nov-Dec). Schools.

Shinewater Park, Larkspur Drive, is newly developed and has lakes, beautiful countryside walks, lovely views to the South Downs, a children's playground, basketball and an Xtreme skatepark. **Open all year.**

Eastbourne(near), **Beachy Head Countryside Centre,** 01323 737273. Learning can be fun if you listen to tales from the talking shepherd, explore marine life in the rock pool, use the Micrarium and touch screen computer, see the video show and much more. Open daily, 10am-4pm (5pm Easter-Sept). **Open all year.**

Birling Gap Beach, off the A259. A steep climb down cliff steps leads you to this sheltered cove, which is set against a backdrop of white cliffs. **Open all year.**

Long Man of Wilmington, is a huge hill carving, surrounded in mystery, that has baffled archaeologists and historians for hundreds of years. Situated S of Wilmington village, there are public footpaths to the base and top of the figure and information boards at the car park and bottom of the hill. Schools **Open all year.**

South Downs Way, www.nationaltrails.gov.uk is a long distance (106 miles) bridleway for walkers, cyclists and horseriders, following the South Downs ridge from Eastbourne to Hampshire. Car parks are sited along the route. **Open all year.**

Forest Row, **Ashdown Forest,** www.ashdownforest.org 01342 823583, has acres of heath and woodland with footpaths and fine viewpoints. The Information Centre at Wych Cross has displays on the natural attractions of the forest. Centre open Apr-Sept, Mon-Fri, 2-5pm; Sat & Sun, 11am-5pm, weekends only Oct-Mar. Schools **Open all year.**

Hailsham(near), **Abbot's Wood,** owned by the Forestry Commission, is signposted from the A22 and A27. It is mixed woodland, particularly lovely at bluebell time and there are marked trails, including one to the lake. Picnic area and a rustic adventure play area. **Open all year.**

Hastings, **Alexandra Park,** consists of 120 acres of beautiful gardens, trees and open space. There is a children's playground, lakes and tennis courts. **Open all year.**

Hastings Country Park, 01424 813225, can be reached from the East Hill Cliff Railway or by car via the Fairlight Road. There are over 600 acres of some of the most beautiful coastal scenery and a rich variety of wildlife in different habitats. Visitor Centre open Fri-Wed, 10am-3pm (weather permitting). **Open all year.**

Hastings Museum and Art Gallery, Bohemia Road, 01424 781155, has many interesting exhibits from all over the world. There is a Junior Museum Club for 7-11s. Open Mon-Sat, 10am-5pm, Sun 2-5pm. Schools **Open all year.**

Lifeboat Station, 01424 425502, is on the Old Town Beach, next to the fishing fleet. From the Visitors Centre you can see the all-weather lifeboat in the boathouse, the inshore inflatable lifeboat and the latest launching tractor. Open daily, 10am-5pm, (4pm in Winter). Schools **Open all year.**

Shipwreck Heritage Centre, Rock-a-Nore Road, 01424 437452, aims to illustrate the history of ships and seafaring. You can monitor shipping in the Channel on radar and make a weather forecast from satellite pictures. Open daily, 10.30am-5pm, later in high Summer. Schools **Open all year.**

Heathfield to Hampden Park, **Cuckoo Trail,** 01273 481637, is a 13 mile all weather path for walkers and cyclists which runs along the route of a former railway. There are sculptures and benches along the way. **Open all year.**

Hove, **Hove Lagoon,** near the sea front, on the western side of Hove, is a children's park with sand pit, paddling pool and cafe. A three mile cycle route runs from here to Palace Pier, Brighton. **Open all year.**

Hove Museum and Art Gallery, New Church Road, 01273 292828, houses one of the largest toy collections in England. `Wizard's Attic' an interactive toy gallery has toys and games from around the world. Open Tues-Sat, 10am-5pm, Sun, 2-5pm. Schools **Open all year.**

Hove Park, has plenty of space with basketball and tennis courts for older children, as well as a play area with swings and climbing frame. Cafe. The miniature railway runs on the last Sat in the month and Bank Hol Mons, Mar-Sept. Schools.

Rye, Camber Sands, is a lovely beach for little ones. The golden sands go out for half a mile at low tide, excellent for paddling and sand castles. **Open all year.**

Rye Harbour Nature Reserve is a flat, open and historical area with a network of footpaths. There are guided walks, four bird watching hides and an unmanned Information Centre in the car park. Walk to Camber Castle which is open Jul-Sept, Sat, Sun, 2-5pm. **Open all year.**

Town Salts, is a pleasant place for picnics. There are public bowling greens, a putting green and a fenced children's playground. **Open all year.**

Seaford, Salt's Recreation Ground, has a pitch and putt, tennis courts, two skate parks, a children's play area and a cafe. There are special children's events held in the Summer. **Open all year.**

Seven Sisters Country Park, Exceat, 01323 870280, covering 692 acres of the Cuckmere Valley and part of the Seven Sisters cliffs provides a habitat for a wide variety of natural life. Converted barns house the Park Centre. Centre open Easter-Oct, Mon-Fri, 10.30am-4.30pm, (Sat, Sun and Bank Hols, 5pm), Nov-Easter, Sat & Sun only, 11am-4pm. Schools **Open all year.**

WEST SUSSEX

Ardingly, Ardingly Reservoir lies in a picturesque natural valley, a lovely area for walks and nature study. There is a bird hide with displays for easy identification. **Open all year.**

Arundel, Arundel Park, is a lovely place for walks on the Sussex downland. Rowing boats for hire on Swanbourne Lake, home to many species of waterfowl. **Open all year.**

Arundel(near), Whiteways Countryside Site, at the junction of the A29 and A284, 01243 811533. There are many lovely walks and a cycle path through the woods and grassland. Guide available from cafe. **Open all year.**

Bognor Regis, Hotham Park, 01243 830262, is a woodland park for all seasons. There is a play area for young children, putting green, crazy golf, tennis court, miniature railway, walled garden, cafe and bandstand with performances in the Summer. **Open all year.**

Burgess Hill, Bedelands Farm Nature Reserve, entrance via car park in Maple Drive. There are several marked, circular walks and an opportunity to see a variety of wildlife. **Open all year.**

St. John's Park, off London Road. There is plenty of space for games, a picnic area, adventure playground, skatepark and tennis courts and special children's activity days in the Summer. **Open all year.**

Marle Place, Upper St. John's Road has a lovely children's play area, a scented garden as well as a large multi-use area for games. **Open all year.**

Chichester, Chichester Cathedral, www.chichester-cathedral.org.uk 01243 782595, dating from Norman times, has outstanding architecture, stained glass, furniture and tapestries. Tours held Easter-Sept. Open daily, 7.30am-7pm, (6pm in Winter). Schools **Open all year.**

Chichester District Museum, 29 Little London, 01243 784683. Although small, it houses displays on local geology, archaeology, industry and also the Romans, with artefacts from home and army life. Open Tues-Sat, 10am-5.30pm. Schools **Open all year.**

Chichester Harbour, www.conservancy.co.uk 01243 512301, is an area of outstanding natural beauty. Explore tidal creeks and inlets, spot wildfowl and waders on the salt marshes, or 'boatwatch' as you walk along the shoreline. Chichester Harbour Conservancy offers guided walks with quiz sheets, colouring sheets and wordsearch. Schools **Open all year.**

Clayton, Clayton Windmills, near Hassocks, 01273 843263. The Jack and Jill Windmill Society have lovingly restored Jill Mill and conduct fascinating tours of the beautiful old mill. Open Easter-Sept, Suns & Bank Hol Mons, 2-5pm. School parties midweek by arrangement. Schools.

Crawley, Buchan Country Park, off the A2220, 01293 542088, consists of wood and heathland with a lake and a network of paths. There are picnic and fishing areas, guided walks and family events. The Countryside Centre is open weekend afternoons or by arrangement and has various displays and facilities for visiting schools. Schools **Open all year.**

Tilgate Park and Nature Centre, Titmus Drive, 01293 521168. This lovely park has a playground, maze, walled gardens, craft workshops and a cafe. The Nature Centre is home to both domestic and wild animals. Dray rides, Sat, Sun & most school hols (groups by arrangement). Nature Centre open daily, 10am-6pm (4pm in Winter). Schools **Open all year.**

Cuckfield, Cuckfield Recreation Ground has an enclosed children's playground with a paddling pool, as well as tennis courts and football pitches. **Open all year.**

East Grinstead, East Court, College Lane, is in the heart of the town and offers beautiful views and walks, a large play area, skate park and playing fields. **Open all year.**

Forest Way, 01273 482670, runs from East Grinstead to Groombridge along the route of a disused railway. It is a pretty, peaceful and mainly level track for families to cycle. There are also four well-marked circular walks. Park your car in Forest Row, or there is limited parking at both Hartfield Station and Ham Bridge. **Open all year.**

Mount Noddy Recreation Ground and Centre, has floodlit multi-purpose courts, an 18-hole putting course, children's play area, bowling green and attractive gardens. **Open all year.**

East Wittering(near), Bracklesham Bay Beach, is exceptionally pretty and interesting too, with sharks' teeth and fossils to be found. At low tide, the gently sloping, sandy beach is ideal for young children. **Open all year.**

Hartfield, Pooh Trail, off the B2026. A.A. Milne wrote his famous stories in this village some 75 years ago. Today you can visit the forest playground of Christopher Robin and Winnie the Pooh. Explore The Hundred Acre Wood (Ashdown Forest), before you find the original bridge to play poohsticks. **Open all year.**

Haslemere(near), Blackdown Hill, NT, is the highest point in Sussex and provides stunning views over the surrounding countryside. Explore the many paths through the mixed wood and heathland with information boards and leaflets. There are several car parks. **Open all year.**

Haywards Heath, Beech Hurst Gardens, Butlers Green Road. There is a good playground for younger children, tennis courts, bowling green, putting, a popular miniature steam railway and a restaurant. **Open all year.**

Victoria Park, South Road, provides plenty of open space, multi-purpose courts, a safe enclosed play area with paddling pool, trim trail and occasional activities. **Open all year.**

Henfield, Woods Mill Countryside Centre, Shoreham Road, www.sussexwt.org.uk 01273 492630. Spot nightingales, woodpeckers, dragonflies and many more on nature trails through woodland and lakeside. Special events arranged, telephone for details. Schools **Open all year.**

Horsham, Horsham Museum, 9 The Causeway, 01403 254959, houses many unusual objects including a cabinet of curiosity. Enjoy the History of Childhood and Costume Galleries, with computer access to the collections. Summer holiday activities. Open Mon-Sat, 10am-5pm. Closed Bank Hols. Schools **Open all year.**

Horsham Park, 01403 215491, provides lots of facilities for families with a play area, tennis and basketball courts, skateboard park, maze, coffee shop and scented garden, as well as a pondside walk and beach area. Children's entertainment in Summer hols, Tues, Wed & Thurs pm, plus free live music on the park podium at weekends in Summer. **Open all year.**

Leechpool and Owlbeech Woods, Harwood Road, has 85 acres of ancient woodland, conifers and heathland. There are self-guided trails and a surfaced path. **Open all year.**

Warnham Nature Reserve, Warnham Road (B2237), 01403 256890, is a tranquil nature reserve with a historical hammerpond, reedbeds, woodlands and meadow, as well as bird hides and a nature trail. Visitor Centre open Thurs-Sun, 10am-6pm. School visits arranged Mon-Wed. Summer holiday activities. Café. **Open all year.**

Horsham(near), Southwater Country Park, off the A24, 01403 731218, is a 54 acre park with a network of hard paths providing year round access, excellent for young children and pushchairs. There are two lakes, the largest of which is used for a range of activities. Children will enjoy the enclosed adventure playground as well as the Summer activities and voluntary conservation work. Visitor Centre open Sat, Sun and daily in school hols, 11am-5pm. Schools **Open all year.**

Littlehampton, Littlehampton Museum, Manor House, Church Street, 01903 738100. Enjoy five permanent galleries, including `The Littlehampton Story - BC to CD', the `Sea Room' with over 200 ship models and the `Lens Room', as well as a programme of temporary exhibitions. Open Tues-Sat, 10.30am-4.30pm. Schools **Open all year.**

Norfolk Gardens, 01903 722466, contains tennis courts, pitch and putt and adventure golf. It is separated by a miniature railway from Mewsbrook Park where there is a boating lake. Cafe. **Open all year.**

Poynings, Devils Dyke, is an amazing natural valley which, according to legend, was dug by the Devil. The views are superb, a great place for a picnic and kite flying! **Open all year.**

Selsey, Lifeboat Museum 01243 602833, contains items relating to the history of lifeboats and an audio-visual show. Sea safety demonstrations take place on a Sunday in Aug during `Lifeboat Week', using the lifeboat and helicopter. Open daily, Easter-Sept, 10am-1pm & 2-5pm. Schools.

Siddlesham, Pagham Harbour Local Nature Reserve, 01243 641508, is an attractive natural harbour - a peaceful haven for plants, insects and especially birds. The main car park is off the Chichester to Selsey Road from where there are nature trails. Visitor Centre open Mon, Tues, Thurs, Fri, 10am-1pm, Sat, Sun, 10am-4pm. **Open all year.**

Three Bridges, Worth Way, is a 7 mile walk from Three Bridges, Crawley to East Grinstead. It follows the old railway line and is an excellent route for young families to enjoy cycling. **Open all year.**

Worthing, Beach House Grounds, Lots here for children, with a paddling pool and Peter Pan's playground with its pay-as-you-go rides.

Brooklands Park, near the sea front, has plenty of variety - go-karts, trampolines, miniature railway, playpark, putting, pitch & putt, 9 hole golf course, boating lake and cafe. Lots of open space for walking and picnics. **Open all year.**

Highdown Gardens, Littlehampton Road. Beautiful gardens linked by lots of small paths which are great for younger children to explore. Children's quiz available. A footpath from the car park leads to Highdown Hill which, on a clear day, boasts stunning views across to the Isle of Wight, Chichester, Brighton and Beachy Head. A lovely picnic spot. Gardens open daily 10am-4pm, weekends only in Winter. **Open all year.**

Worthing Museum and Art Gallery, Chapel Road, 01903 239999 (Ext. 1140) weekdays & 01903 221150, Sats. Displays ranging from local archaeology to fashions through the ages. The toys and dolls' houses will delight children. Events held throughout the year. Open Mon-Sat, 10am-5pm. Schools **Open all year.**

Can't find a babysitter?

SitterS
0800 38 900 38

For Evening Babysitters
www.sitters.co.uk

Evening Babysitters with Professional Childcare Experience

Now you can find mature, friendly and reliable evening babysitters, available at short notice. For your reassurance we interview each babysitter in person and check all references thoroughly.

All Sitters babysitters have professional childcare experience and most are local authority registered childminders or professionally qualified nursery nurses.

How does Sitters' service work

When you make a booking we arrange for a babysitter to attend at the appointed time. At the end of the evening you pay the babysitter for the hours they have worked. Babysitting rates start from £4.40 per hour and vary depending on your area. There are no additional charges for travelling costs and all bookings are for a minimum of 4 hours.

Each time you book a babysitter we charge a nominal £4 booking fee to your credit card. You can register with Sitters free! Membership of just £12.75 for 3 months will only be charged <u>after</u> your first sitting. Call us today - less than £1 per week is a small price to ensure your children are in experienced hands.

Experienced Childcarers Needed

Sitters welcomes applications from suitable babysitters. You will need to be over 21, have professional childcare experience, your own transport and immaculate references. For more information and to register your interest phone 0800 38 900 38 or visit www.sitters.co.uk.

For more information, phone us FREE today or

0800 38 900 38
or visit us at www.sitters.co.uk
Please quote Ref: LET'S GO

Recruitment & Employment Confederation

We're in  YELLOW PAGES

INVESTOR IN PE

Trips & Transport

It is a real adventure for children to go on a journey and to experience other forms of transport, either as an organised excursion or trip, or trying out other vehicles for themselves. You can hire boats or bikes, take bus tours or ride stream trains. Enjoy getting away from the car!

BOAT HIRE

EAST SUSSEX

Bodiam, Bodiam Ferry Company, 01797 253838. Trips on the River Rother between Bodiam Castle and Newenden Bridge, operate Wed, Sat, Sun, May-Jun, daily Jul-Aug. Tearoom and rowing boats to hire. Price C.

Brighton Marina, Marina Water Tours, Pagoda Berth, 07958246414, offers regular harbour, sea trips and pier cruises in the Summer and by request to the end of Oct. Price P.

Eastbourne, Allchorn Pleasure Boats, The Pier, www.allchornpleasureboats.co.uk 01323 410606. 45 minute return trips to view the white cliffs and the 100 year old lighthouse, operate from May-Sept, weather permitting. Price C.

Lamberhurst(near), Bewl Cruises, Bewl Water, 01892 890171/890661. Cruises operate from the Visitors Centre. Daily, Easter-Sept. Price B and specials.

Newhaven, Hoverspeed, 08705 240241. Regular catamaran services to Dieppe in France take about two hours and dock close to the historic town centre leaving time to shop and browse before returning same day. Operates daily, Mar-Sept. Price G.

WEST SUSSEX

Chichester, Chichester Canal Trading Company, Basin Road, 01243 771363. Return cruises from the canal basin to Donnington. Schools Open all year Price A.

Itchenor, Chichester Harbour Water Tours, 01243 670504. Trips around Chichester Harbour. Schools.

Littlehampton, Kingfisher Cruises, 01903 723666/07814183824. A covered boat runs to Ford Marina daily and hourly in the Summer. Longer trips can be booked for groups all year round. Open all year Price B.

Loxwood(near), Wey and Arun Canal Trust, Billingshurst, 01403 752403. Narrowboat trips along the Canal, negotiating a lock on the way. Operates at weekends, Apr-Oct. Schools Price A/B/G.

BUS TRIPS

Stagecoach South East, www.stagecoachbus.com 0845 121 0170. Exploring the south by bus is excellent value and avoids the inconvenience of finding a parking space in some of the most popular tourist areas. The Stagecoach Coastliner, route 700, is a frequent service between Southsea and Brighton and provides links across the south including Portsmouth Hard for connections to the Isle of Wight. The One-day Goldrider tickets offer unlimited travel on all Stagecoach buses across the South East. Also available are a range of combined entrance and travel tickets for a number of the best attractions in Sussex, including Butlins at Bognor Regis, Weald & Downland Open Air Museum, near Chichester and Brighton Sea Life Centre. Available in adult, child and family versions, all tickets provide great savings on paying for the bus and entrance separately. Telephone or visit the website for details of other Stagecoach routes, the Coastliner or ticket information. **Check out page 30.**

CYCLE HIRE

EAST SUSSEX

Forest Row, **Futurecycles,** Lower Square, 01342 822847.
Heathfield, **Cycle Revival,** Oxford House, 01435 866118.
Seaford, **Cuckmere Cycle Company,** Seven Sisters Country Park, 01323 870310.
Rye, Rye Hire, **Cyprus Place,** 01797 223033.

WEST SUSSEX

Fishbourne, **Barreg Cycles,** 01243 786104.
Horsham(near), **Southwater Cycles,** Southwater, 01403 732561.
Worthing(near), **Splash Mountain Bikes,** Findon, 01903 872300.

DRIVING

WEST SUSSEX

East Grinstead, Leisure Pursuits, Ashurst Wood, www.leisurepursuits.co.uk 01342 825522, organise off-road activities for young would-be drivers. Groups of 3-36 children (6+ yrs) can enjoy two exhilarating hours with all necessary instruction and supervision whilst driving. Groups choose three activities from a list that includes the Jungle Run, Meadow Meander and other 4x4 courses, time trials, relays and obstacle courses on quad bikes, grass-track rally-karts and purpose-built fun vehicles, the Dizzymobile and Periscope Peril. From the age of 14, Driver Training sessions on 4-wheel drive jeeps cover basic driving techniques, either for individuals or up to three people in one vehicle. Please telephone for prices and bookings. Birthdays **Check out page 30.**

TRAIN TRIPS

South Central Trains, www.southcentraltrains.co.uk 0870 830 6000, Customer Services. Many Sussex attractions are easily accessible from local South Central stations (Brighton Express to and from London Victoria in under one hour). To celebrate the sheer diversity, interest and value of what is available, South Central produce a Summer Guide that is full of ideas for places to go and unusual people and events to see. Highlights this year are exclusive 2:1 Summer offers at Brighton Sea Life, Royal Pavilion, Arundel Castle and more, plus an unbeatable package from London Original one of the best sightseeing bus experiences, with free circular river cruise (worth £7) and a traditional fish and chips lunch (worth £5.95). All this and more can be viewed at www.placestogopeopletosee.co.uk. For Winter (Oct-May) there are great deals called `2 for 1' that include entry to top London attractions, theatre, restaurant and hotel discounts. Not to be missed are the combined meal and show offers, including blockbusters such as Les Miserables, Chicago, Fame, Bombay Dreams and many others. **Check out outside back cover.**

EAST SUSSEX

Bodiam, Kent and East Sussex Steam Railway, www.kesr.org.uk 01580 765155, runs from Tenterden, just over the border, to Bodiam Castle and back. Trains run mainly in the Summer with Special Christmas trips. Telephone for timetable. Schools **Price C.**

Brighton, Volks Railway, Madeira Drive, 01273 292718, is the world's first electric railway opened in 1883. The carriages powered by their original Victorian motors, run for just over a mile along Brighton's seafront past the fishermen's boats. Trains leave every 15 minutes from the Aquarium, Marina and Paston Place Station, which is located in the centre. The journey time is 12 mins. Each train holds 80 people. Schools can attend a free talk on Victorian railways, by arrangement, and an educational pack is available. There is ample parking opposite the railway. Open daily, Easter-Sept, 11.15am-5pm, (Sat-Sun, 6pm.) Schools Price A **Check out page 30.**

Eastbourne, Dotto Trains. These 'trains' run along the promenade from Hollywell to Sovereign Park stopping at all the attractions en route. Operate daily, Easter-Oct.

Eastbourne Miniature Steam Railway Adventure Park, Southbourne Lake, Lottbridge Drove. www.emsr.co.uk 01323 520229. Travel on coaches pulled by a miniature steam locomotive. Café with tea garden. Open daily, Easter-Sept, 10am-5pm, Sat, Sun in Oct. Schools Price B **Check out `Adventure' chapter and page 40.**

Hastings, Cliff Railways. The East Hill Railway is the steepest in the country, linking the Country Park to Rock-a-Nore Road. 01424 781040. The West Hill Railway links the castle and caves to the old town shopping area and sea front. 01424 781030. Both railways are open daily, Easter-Sept, 10am-5.30pm. Oct-Easter, 11am-4pm. **Open all year.**

Isfield, Lavender Line, near Uckfield, 01825 750515, runs steam or diesel trains with unlimited rides on day of visit. Spend the day in the Family Garden, see the old signal box with levers to pull or have a light meal at the Buffet. Special events include `Santa' trains. Operate Suns all year, Sat & Sun, Jun-Aug (also Wed in Aug) and Dec. Birthdays Price B.

Sheffield Park, The Bluebell Railway, www.bluebell-railway.co.uk 01825 720800. Experience the sights and sounds of the age of steam on this round trip, boarding trains at Sheffield Park, Kingscote or Horsted Keynes, 1930s and 1950s period stations. Open daily, May-Sept and school hols, Sat and Sun only, Oct-May. Schools Birthdays **Open all year** Price C.

WEST SUSSEX

Bognor Regis, Land Train, 01243 842099. Runs from Butlins to the Regis Centre. Easter-Oct, daily, weather permitting. Also runs from Bognor Pier to Marine Park Gardens in Summer hols and weekends, weather permitting. Price A.

Littlehampton, Land Train, 01243 842099. Runs from Smarts Amusements to Norfolk Gardens, Easter-Oct, daily, weather permitting. Price A.

ROYAL BOTANIC GARDENS KEW
WAKEHURST PLACE

Wakehurst Place

Kew's country garden

Near Ardingly, West Sussex   24hr information   01444 894 066   www.kew.org

Farms, Wildlife & Nature Parks

All children love animals and there are many species to see in Sussex, either in farm surroundings, nature parks or aquariums. All places listed in this chapter have admission charges but there are other places of natural interest, which are free to visit. Check out the `Free Places' chapter.

EAST SUSSEX

Alfriston, Drusillas Park, off the A27, www.drusillas.co.uk 01323 874100, winner of the SEETB Visitor Attraction Award, is an excellent small zoo where you come nose to nose with nature. There are over 150 animal species in naturalistic environments, all with low-level viewing. The walk-through Rodrigues Fruit Bat enclosure allows you to see at close quarters these captivating creatures, and an imaginative exhibition includes many fascinating facts about British bats. Children can climb inside a dome at the Meerkat Mound and get really close to the animals. Pet World contains everything from rabbits and guinea pigs to snakes, spiders and geckos, while the Petting Barn provides an opportunity to stroke and groom a variety of friendly goats and sheep. Enjoy a creepy crawly experience in Millennium Bugs and don't miss penguin feeding times daily at 11.30am and 4pm. Children can have great fun in Playland with over an acre of creative climbing, jumping and swinging equipment - thoughtfully separated for different age groups. Indoors, the Playbarn is a complete playground for older children and the Toddler Village and Toy Stables are a great hit with under 6s. The Wacky Workshop, Panning for Gold and a huge Bouncy Castle are open at weekends and school holidays. Keeper talks emphasise the importance of conservation and the Maasai Exhibition shows how a different culture relates to the animals and the environment around them. In addition, there are beautiful gardens, train rides, Zoolympics, the Discovery Centre, Jungle Adventure Golf, Explorers Lagoon, Vertical Limit (climbing wall), Mokomo's Jungle Rock, Explorers Restaurant, Oasis Café and five shops. Drusillas offers a fun and educational day out for everyone. The Park is fully accessible for wheelchair users. Open daily, 10am-6pm, (5pm in Winter). Schools Birthdays **Open all year** Price D **Check out inside front cover.**

Beckley, Farm World, Great Knelle Farm, www.farmworld-rye.co.uk 01797 260250, is a relaxed working farm where visitors are encouraged to help feed the animals. Pony and tractor rides, a BMX course and metal detecting in the woods. Open daily in school hols. Telephone for opening times. **Price B.**

Brighton, Brighton Sea Life Centre, Marine Parade, www.sealife.co.uk 01273 604234. There are thousands of sea creatures to see here. A walk through one of England's longest underwater tunnel brings you face to face with marine life, from shrimps to sharks, octopus to eels. There are feeding demonstrations and talks. Restaurant and gift shop. Open daily, 10am-5pm. Schools Birthdays **Open all year** Price C.

Ditchling, Stoneywish Nature Reserve and Tearoom, Spatham Lane, 01273 843498. See the farm animals, spend imaginative playtime at the wigwam, tractor, swings and slides, or have a picnic in the play area. There is also a woodland walk. Open daily, 9.30am-5pm, 4pm in Winter. No charge for entrance to tearoom. Schools **Open all year** Price B.

East Dean, Seven Sisters Sheep Centre, Birling Manor Farm, 01323 423302, on the road to Beachy Head, is home to 47 different breeds of sheep. Demonstrations on lambing, shearing, milking and opportunities to bottle feed lambs held in season. Tractor and trailer rides. Animals can be brought to visit children at school, by arrangement. Café. Open 6th Mar-3rd May & 3rd Jul-5th Sept, Mon-Fri, 2-5pm, Sat, Sun, Bank & school hols, 11am-5pm. Schools Birthdays Price B.

Forest Row(near), Ashdown Forest Llama Park, Wych Cross, www.llamapark.co.uk 01825 712040. Stroll around the farm trail and see the breeding herds of llamas and alpacas. Visit the museum where you can learn about their history as well as information on other fibre producing animals and plants. Play area, picnic tables, gift shop and café. Open daily, 10am-5pm. Schools **Open all year** Price B.

Hadlow Down, Wilderness Wood, on the A272, www.wildernesswood.co.uk 01825 830509, is a working wood, especially lovely at bluebell time. It has many paths, a woodland trail, picnic places, barbecue stands for hire and an adventure play area. Shop and tearoom. Holiday activities and special `Castaway' birthday parties can be arranged. Open daily, 10am-5.30pm, dusk if earlier. Schools Birthdays **Open all year** Price A.

Hailsham(near), Mohair Centre, Chiddingly, Brickfield Farm, www.mohaircentre.co.uk 01825 872457, offers plenty of fun with small animals to handle, larger farm animals to see and lambs and kids in Spring. There is an after school club and workshops in school holidays, by arrangement. Open Suns only, 10am-4.30pm. Tearoom open in Summer. Schools Birthdays **Open all year** Price A.

Hastings, Underwater World, Rock-a-Nore Road, 01424 718776, offers a unique opportunity to experience the secret lives of native marine species. Walk through the underwater tunnel and enjoy a panoramic view of sharks and rays and then discover Neptune's Nursery where many fish are born and reared. Open daily, Mar-Oct, 10am-5pm, Nov-Feb, 11am-4pm. Schools Birthdays **Open all year** Price B.

Lamberhurst(near), Bewl Water, www.bewl.co.uk 01892 890661, is the largest area of inland water in the SE. Cruise aboard the Swallow, walk or ride the Round Reservoir Route and enjoy the watersports. Restaurant, shop and summer events. Open 9am-sunset. Schools **Open all year** Price A.

Lewes(near), Bentley Wildfowl and Motor Museum, Halland, www.bentley.org.uk 01825 840573, has a lot to offer the whole family. See many different species of wildfowl, including black swans, flamingos and peacocks. There are gardens, Bentley House, the Motor Museum, an adventure playground and a miniature railway (Sat, Sun and Bank Hols, Easter-Sept). Open daily, mid Mar-end Oct, 10.30am-4.30pm. House open Apr-Oct, 12noon-5pm. Open weekends only Nov, Feb and early Mar. Schools Birthdays Price B.

Middle Farm, near Firle, www.middlefarm.com 01323 811411, is a large working farm with lots for children to enjoy, farmyard and small animals to see, daily milking sessions of the Jersey cows and a play area. Bring your own picnic or eat in the restaurant. Open daily, 10am-5pm. Schools Birthdays **Open all year** Price A.

Ringmer, Raystede Centre for Animal Welfare, 01825 840252, welcomes visitors who appreciate the Centre's priority for the well being of animals. Domestic pets, birds and exotic animals are cared for here and there is also a wildlife sanctuary and shop. Parking charge and entry by donation. Open daily, 10am-4pm. Schools **Open all year** Price A.

Robertsbridge(near), Sedlescombe Organic Vineyard, 01580 830715, on the B2244 N of Hastings. Follow the nature trail through vineyards and woodland using the informative guide and numbered points. Take a picnic, entry includes wine-tasting for adults and fruit juices for children. Open daily, Apr-Dec, 10am-5.30pm. Sat-Sun only Jan-Mar, 12noon-5pm. Schools **Open all year** Price A.

Uckfield, Heaven Farm, Furners Green, on the A275 between Danehill and the Bluebell Railway, www.heavenfarm.co.uk 01825 790226, has a woodland nature trail, particularly pretty in Spring and Autumn, and a small farming museum. Tearoom in stables. Open daily, Mar-Nov, 10am-5.30pm, (museum times vary). Schools Price A.

Uckfield(near), Sheffield Park Garden, NT, 01825 790231, is a magnificent landscaped garden with lakes and waterfalls and lots of paths, wonderful for exploring. Children's trail guide and special events throughout the year. Open 1st Jan-27th Feb, Sat & Sun only, 10.30am-4pm,

2nd Mar-31st Oct, Tues-Sun and Bank Hol Mons, 10.30am-6pm, (4pm 2nd Nov-23rd Dec). **Open all year** Price B.

Whitesmith, The Farmyard, N of Hailsham off the A22 at the crossroads, 01825 872317, welcomes families. Children can climb in to stroke the rabbits and chickens and near-by are geese, goats, donkeys and horses. There is a Nature Trail and picnic area. Open Easter-Oct, Mon-Fri, 2-5pm, Sat, 10am-5pm. Schools Price A.

TRAVEL GAMES

For every letter of the alphabet starting with A
you need to spot an object beginning with that letter
before moving on to the next letter.

You can play this individually or as a team.

WEST SUSSEX

Ardingly, Wakehurst Place, NT, www.kew.org 01444 894066 (24 hr information line), on the B2028, is otherwise known as 'Kew in the Country'. These marvellous gardens and woodlands cover over 300 acres with endless variety and areas of beauty in all seasons. Children will enjoy exploring the many paths and will love the pond, lake and wetland areas with their resident wildfowl. The country mansion houses a gift shop and there is also a restaurant. The Millennium Seed Bank holds the seeds of some 90% of UK plants and this conservation initiative aims to save the most highly endangered plant species around the world from extinction. Interactive computers explain the sorting and storage process and there is easy viewing into the laboratories to see work in progress. Open daily from 10am, closing times vary throughout the year. (Seed Bank closes 1 hour before gardens.) Children under 17 are admitted free. Schools **Open all year** Price B **Check out page 32.**

Arundel, The Wildfowl and Wetlands Centre, www.wwt.org.uk 01903 883355, is the perfect place for a different family day out. There are 60 acres of ponds, lakes and reedbeds with many hundred varieties of the most spectacular wildfowl. With walkways, paths, observation hides and a viewing lounge, children will enjoy getting nose to beak with nature, as many birds are so tame they feed straight from the hand. Most weekends are marked with special events or activities and during half term there are additional discovery and hands-on activities, but it is worth telephoning beforehand for details. Visitor Centre, restaurant and shop. Open daily, 9.30am-5.30pm (4.30pm in Winter). Schools **Open all year** Price B **Check out page 36.**

Ashington, Holly Gate Cactus Garden, Billingshurst Road, on the B2133, www.hollygatecactus.co.uk 01903 892930, will fascinate everyone. Over 30,000 plants ranging from the minute to the enormous and some up to 100 years old. Look out for the mother-in-law's seat! Picnic area. Open daily, 9am-5pm (4pm Nov-Jan). Schools **Open all year** Price A.

Birdham, Earnley Butterflies and Gardens, 133 Almodington Lane, 01243 512637, offers the chance to see exotic birds and butterflies. Themed gardens lead to a picnic and play area and new for 2004 is Noah's Ark, a rescue centre, housing small and amazing creatures! Crazy golf course. Open daily mid Mar-end Oct, 10am-6pm. Schools Price B.

Sussex Falconry Centre, Wophams Lane, 01243 512472, has numerous different species of owls, as well as hawks, eagles and falcons. See their agility at set flying times with intermittent displays. Open daily from Mar-Sept, 10am-5pm. Price A.

Chichester, West Dean Gardens, off the A286, www.westdean.org.uk 01243 818210. Set within sweeping lawns, these delightful gardens have a Victorian Walled Kitchen Garden with thirteen original glasshouses, 35 acres of ornamental grounds, a landscaped park, arboretum and a parkland walk. Visitor centre, restaurant, shop and regular events. Open Mar-Oct, 11am-5pm (10.30am May-Sept) Schools Price B.

East Grinstead, Deers Leap Park, www.deersleappark.co.uk 01342 325858, is a great place to go cycling or walking. This working farm has mountain bike trails for all abilities including a total of six miles of main track and a further four miles of graded woodland trails. You can take your own bikes or hire from an extensive range. There are footpaths, picnic areas and barbecue facilities so whether cycling or walking, you can enjoy the 230 acres of beautiful countryside. An on-site shop sells bicycles, parts and accessories and the kiosk sells refreshments. Open daily, Mar-Sept, 9am-6pm; Oct-Feb, Sat, Sun & school hols, 9am-5pm (Mon-Fri, bookings only). Schools Birthdays **Open all year** Price C **Check out page 36.**

Faygate, Holmbush Farm World, near Horsham, www.holmbushfarm.co.uk 01293 851110, will delight the young with its unusual mix of animals, rheas and ferrets, as well as traditional farm animals. Children learn about the farm and enjoy the daily milking demonstrations, tractor and trailer rides and goat races. Let them burn off excess energy in the bale maze (under 8s only), extensive indoor and outdoor play areas and woodland walk, while grown-ups can recharge their batteries in the tearoom. Special events include sheep shearing, sheepdog demonstrations, falconry displays and visits from snakes and reptiles. There is a gift shop and farm shop. Open daily, Mar-Oct, 10am-5.30pm. Schools Birthdays Price B **Check out page 36.**

Handcross, High Beeches Gardens, www.highbeeches.com 01444 400589, are home to a variety of wildlife in a peaceful woodland setting. Special events in Summer. Tea rooms. Open Apr-Jun, Sept-Oct, Thurs-Tues, Jul-Aug, Mon-Tues, Thurs-Fri, Sun, 1-5pm. Price A.
Nymans, NT, 01444 400321, are beautiful gardens with vibrant displays of Spring, Summer and Autumn colour, woodland walks and many rare and exotic plants. Several rooms in the house are open to visitors. Gardens open 18th Feb-31st Oct, Wed-Sun, 11am-6pm, 6th Nov-20th Feb, Sat-Sun, 11am-5pm. **Open all year** Price B.

Haywards Heath, Borde Hill Garden, Park & Playground, www.bordehill.co.uk 01444 450326, offers fun for all the family. The adventure playground with its rope bridges and wooden climbers is both fun and challenging. Children can explore the pirate ship, the fort and tree top walk. Let off steam in the picturesque parkland or have a picnic by the lakes, refreshments are available from the tearooms. Learn to fish or visit the Garden with its glorious 'garden rooms'. Events held throughout the year, including activities during Aug (Mon-Fri, 2-5pm) and Oct half-term, such as face painting, juggling skills, tile painting, tractor rides and much more. Open daily, 10am-6pm (or dusk). Schools **Open all year** Price B **Check out page 36.**

Horsham, Huxley's Birds of Prey Centre, 01403 273458, entrance through Hilliers Garden Centre, is a collection of Birds of Prey viewed at close quarters in large landscaped aviaries, typical of their natural habitat. Flying displays with hands-on experiences held regularly. Open Wed-Mon, 11am-5pm, Sun only during Oct-Mar. Schools **Open all year** Price B.

Hurstpierpoint, Washbrooks Farm Centre, Brighton Road, www.washbrooks.co.uk 01273 832201, is a relaxed, friendly, family-run farm where children have the freedom to observe farm animals at close quarters, some of which are under cover. There are many other attractions, including an outdoor adventure playground and an indoor heated play area, party room and facilities. Take a picnic and relax in the beautiful surroundings or enjoy light refreshments available all day from the tearooms. There is also a Farm Shop selling a variety of gifts, toys and preserves. Children's parties can be arranged and other groups are warmly welcomed. Open daily, 9.30am-5pm. Schools Birthdays **Open all year** Price B **Check out page 38.**

Lancing(near), Coombes Farm Tours, Church Farm, www.coombes.co.uk 01273 452028, offer pre-booked groups and families enjoyable and educational tours on the tractor and trailer to see animals grazing, arable farming and conservation areas. Tours in Aug, Tues, Thurs, Sun at 2.30pm. The lambing yard is open to visitors during Mar and Apr. Open Mar-mid Oct during daylight hours. Schools Birthdays Price B.

Lower Beeding, Leonardslee Gardens, www.leonardslee.com 01403 891212, has 240 acres of beautiful gardens and woodland, home to both deer and wallabies. A wild flower trail meanders around the many lakes and streams. Entrance charges higher in May when the rhododendrons and azaleas are at their peak. Open daily, Apr-Oct, 9.30am-6pm. Price B.

Pulborough, Pulborough Brooks RSPB Nature Reserve, on the A283 to Storrington, www.rspb.org.uk 01798 875851, is a reserve for bird watching, wildlife walks and scenic views. The Visitor Centre has information displays and a countryside classroom. Tearoom and shop. Open daily, 10am-5pm. Nature trail, 9am-dusk. Schools **Open all year** Price A.

Wisborough Green, Fishers Farm Park, Newpound Lane, www.fishersfarmpark.co.uk 01403 700063. This multi award-winning visitor attraction is ideally suited for 2-11 year olds and a unique combination of rural farmyard and dynamic adventure play. An all-inclusive entrance fee covers all activities. There are animals to touch, pony and tractor rides and a combine harvester ride! Enjoy theatre shows and indoor Playzones. The wonderful outdoor adventure play areas include bumper boats, climbing wall, quad bikes, spider's web, fort, slides, junior tractors and trampolines. Visit the beach and sandy shore with decked promenade, bouncy castles and a giant bouncy slide. Restaurant and outside refreshments. Open daily, 10am-5pm. Schools Birthdays **Open all year** Price D **Check out below.**

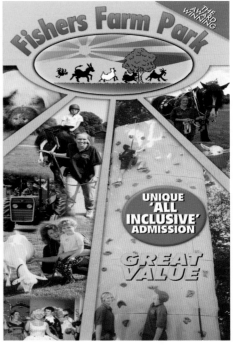

Adventure & Fun

Quite a medley here, with a strong emphasis on fun and play, rides and thrills. This chapter includes play centres, fun activities and unusual themed venues such as laser games, water fun parks and maize mazes.

EAST SUSSEX

Bexhill, Bexhill Leisure Pool, Ravenside Retail Park, 01424 731508. Have fun at the beach area with the wave machine and enjoy a ride on the flume. Open daily but check for wave pool times. **Open all year** Price B.

Brighton, Candy Castle, Enterprise Point, Melbourne Street, www.candycastleplay.co.uk 01273 276060. This multi-level fantasy play centre for under 10s has a Creepy Pit, Spook Room and Sky Glide as well as a separate toddlers' soft play area and bouncy castle. Open daily, 10am-6pm. Closed some Bank Hols. Birthdays **Open all year** Price A.
Charlie Chalk Fun Factory, The Sportsman, Withdean Sports Complex, 01273 330055. Indoor soft play adventure area with ball pool, rigging, slides and tunnels. Birthdays **Open all year** Price A.
Peter Pan's Leisure Park, Madeira Drive, has children's amusements. Open daily, Easter-Sept, 10am-late and Winter weekends. Price P .

Eastbourne, Fort Fun, at the eastern end of Royal Parade, 01323 642833, is an outdoor play complex for children up to age 12. Open Easter-Oct, daily in school hols, weekends only in term time, 10am-6pm. **Rockies Adventureland** is an indoor soft play area, open daily. **Fun Karts** offers the chance to test your driving skills, opening times as for Fort Fun. Birthdays Price B.
Laserquest, Lloyd's Lanes, Broadwater Way, Hampden Park, www.laserquest.co.uk 01323 506007. Zap your opponents before they zap you! Open Mon-Fri, 3-10pm, Sat, Sun, 10am-10pm. Birthdays **Open all year** Price A/B.
Eastbourne Miniature Steam Railway Adventure Park, Lottbridge Drove, www.emsr.co.uk 01323 520229, SEETB Visitor Attraction of the Year 2002, is a family run park with lots of variety. Take a ride on the miniature steam railway or walk the nature trail. Children will enjoy exploring the willow maze and trying out the large adventure playground; there is a Tots Village in the woods for little ones. The indoor and outdoor coin-operated model railways are fun for young train enthusiasts. Café with tea garden. Open daily, Easter-Sept, 10am-5pm. Sat, Sun in Oct. Schools Price B **Check out `Trips' chapter and page 40.**
The Sovereign Centre, Royal Parade. 01323 738822, has a fun pool with a wave machine and flumes. Telephone for opening times and prices. Birthdays **Open all year.**

Hailsham, Knockhatch Adventure Park, www.knockhatch.com 01323 442051, on the A22 just N of Eastbourne, is set in 80 acres of lovely Sussex countryside. The excellent variety of activities includes free fall slide, toboggan run, bouncy castles, a sandpit for younger children, indoor and outdoor adventure playgrounds, woodland trail and much more. Enjoy close encounters with the animal kingdom and maybe meet a friendly eagle or funny vulture. The birds of prey perform daily flying displays and participants can marvel at the owls as they swoop down to perch on a gloved hand! For an extra charge, try Go Karts (weather permitting) or the Quantum Quest outdoor laser game. Open Easter-Oct, Sat, Sun; Jun-Aug, and school hols all year, daily, 10am-5.30pm. Schools Birthdays **Open all year** Price C **Check out page 40.**

Hastings, Clambers Play Centre, White Rock Gardens, www.clambers.co.uk 01424 423778 has an indoor and outdoor area. Inside is the big, bumpy slide, the commando run and sound machines, while outside are the climbing frames, playhouses and paddling pool in Summer. Open daily, 9.30am-6pm. Birthdays Price A.

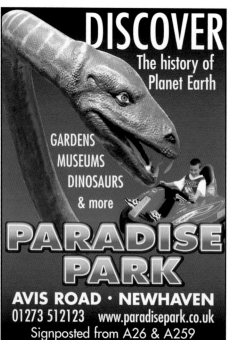

40

The Flamingo Family Fun Park, 01424 715133, offers various amusements. Open days and times as weather permits. Price P.

Hove, **Megazone,** King Alfred Leisure Centre, Kingsway, 01273 779789 for space-age laser fun. Open Mon-Fri, 4-9.30pm, Sat,Sun, 10am-9pm. Birthdays **Open all year** Price B.

Lewes(near), **Kingston,** Spring Barn Farm, www.maizemazes.com 01273 488450, has a fun maze to explore during the Summer. Telephone for opening times and prices.

Newhaven, **Brewsters Fun Factory,** The Drove, Avis Road, 01273 612356. Indoor adventure area for children up to 1.4m with a ball pool, rigging, slides and tunnels. Additional activities include play stations, juggling, face painting and lots more. Separate toddler area. Open daily, 11am-9pm (Fri-Sat, 10pm). Birthdays **Open all year** Price A.

Paradise Park, Avis Road, www.paradisepark.co.uk 01273 512123 (24hr Info. Line: 01273 616006). Discover our amazing past and colourful history through the ages. A new Dinosaur Park gives an insight into life in Sussex millions of years ago. See the fabulous collections of fossils, minerals & crystals and explore the Sussex History Trail as it meanders through the delightful water gardens, with handcrafted models of Sussex landmarks. Enjoy the indoor gardens at this ideal all weather venue. Garden and gift shop, Terrace Café, crazy golf, miniature railway and children's amusements. Open daily, 9am-6pm. Schools Birthdays **Open all year** Price A/B **Check out page 40**.

Seaford, **Dino's Funland,** Downs Leisure Centre, Sutton Road, 01323 490011, is a soft play centre for under 8s with a bouncy castle, dinosaur 'eggs' and shapes, and in the Summer, a fun house and slide as well as a ball pit. Telephone for opening times and prices. Birthdays **Open all year.**

St. Leonards-on-Sea, **Brewsters Fun Factory,** The Windmill, John Macaddam Way, 01424 754070. Indoor adventure area for children up to 1.4m with a ball pool, rigging, slides and tunnels. Open daily, 12noon-9pm with Mother and Toddler mornings, Mon, Wed, Fri, 9am-11.30am. Birthdays **Open all year** Price A.

WEST SUSSEX

Bognor Regis, Butlins, 01243 822445, is a holiday complex, but you can visit for an action-packed day with plenty to amuse children of all ages, including some amazing water rides. Open daily, 10am-8pm (last admission 4pm). Birthdays Price C.

Burgess Hill, Antics, The Triangle Leisure Centre, 01444 876000, is a themed adventure soft play area on three levels, designed for children up to 1.48m. It includes ball pond, tunnel, tumble tower, bash bags and more. There are also amazing water rapids and flumes to enjoy in the leisure pool. Telephone for opening times. Birthdays **Open all year** Price P.

CJ's Playland, Braybon Business Park, Consort Way, www.cjsplayland.co.uk 01444 239991 is a multi level soft play area with mazes, rope and v-bridges, pull swings, log climbs, slides, push balls and more. There are two separate areas for younger children and crawlers. Café. Open daily, 10am-6pm. Birthdays **Open all year** Price A.

Chichester, Adventure Warehouse, Terminus Road Industrial Estate, 01243 839455. This exciting indoor adventure play centre is suitable for children of all ages (height restrictions apply). Have fun on three large inflatables, Shark Slide, Gorilla Mountain and Pirate Ship. The adventure area has lots to enjoy, with a circular slide, squeeze-throughs and more. There is also a separate toddler area, café and gift shop selling educational books and toys. An excellent venue for children's parties, with each guest taking home a party bag and present. Open daily, Mon-Fri, 9.30am-6pm, Sat, Sun, 10am-6pm. In term time only the main play area is used for toddler mornings, Mon, Wed & Fri, 9.30am-1pm. Birthdays **Open all year** Price A **Check out page 40**.

Visiting Relations? Going On Holiday? Gift For A Friend?

LET'S GO WITH THE CHILDREN

Crawley, Arctic Jungle, Denvale Trade Park, www.arcticjungle.co.uk 01293 614999. Enter the Ice Cave to a Jungle themed Playframe with up to four levels and over 60 different play elements and 7 slides. Then move on to the Thunderdome and Fun Guns, hitting mural targets with soft balls, but watch out for the Ball Dumper, it can suddenly rain balls on the unsuspecting! Or attempt the 7.5m high wall climb and then chill out in the Arctic Zone which includes the Arctic Café. Birthday parties are held in themed rooms, each with a `throne' and reached by crossing the Arctic Jungle Bridge, only accessible to partygoers! Height restrictions apply. Open Tues-Sun, 10am-6pm. Birthdays **Open all year** Price A **Check out page 44.**

Horsham, The Pavilions in the Park, Hurst Road, 01403 219200. Have indoor and outdoor fun, all year round on the flume ride, bubble beds and moving water channels. Alternatively, 2-11 year olds can spend time in the soft play area with its ball pool and wavy slide, ball blower, dark tunnel, sticky shape area or climb up to the jungle section! Café and soft area for under 2s. Under 4s to be accompanied by an adult in the soft play area. Telephone for opening times and prices. **Open all year.**

Littlehampton, Harbour Park, on the seafront, 01903 721200, fun rides and games with a maritime theme. Soft play area. Telephone for opening times as some areas open only if weather permitting. Birthdays **Open all year** Price P.

Selsey, Little Monkeys, Green Lawns Caravan Site, 01243 601169, is a jungle-themed indoor play area and an outdoor play garden for children up to age 8. Bouncy castle in the Summer. Open daily, 10am-5.30pm. Birthdays **Open all year** Price A.

Rowlands Castle(near), Standstead Park, www.standstedpark.co.uk 02392 412265 has a traditional maize maze to explore in the Summer.

Worthing, Amazon Adventure, Worthing Leisure Centre, 01903 502237, is a soft play centre with snake slide and ball pool suitable for children up to 1.5m. Open daily in school hols, Mon-Fri, 9.30-11.30am, 1.30-5.30pm, Sat-Sun, 9am-12noon, 2-4pm. Telephone for opening times during term time. Birthdays **Open all year** Price A.

Fun Junction, Stoke Abbott Road, 01903 238877, is a rainforest themed indoor adventure playground, for children up to 1.48m in height. The large soft play area includes slides, ball pools, tunnels and separate play areas for different age groups. Or enjoy a laser game at Quazar. Open daily, 10am-6pm. Birthdays **Open all year** Price A.

The Lido, 01903 213486, is on the promenade and offers family fun and entertainment with amusements, rides for children, video games, restaurant and coffee shop. Open daily, Apr-Sept; Sat, Sun only Oct-Mar, weather permitting. **Open all year** Price P.

Peter Pan's Playground, Beach House Park, has lots of play equipment and rides to keep younger children amused. Open Easter-Sept, 10am-7pm. Price P.

Turners Hill, Tulleys Farm, www.maizemazes.com 01342 718472 has a wonderful maize maze to enjoy in the Summer. Telephone for opening times and prices.

Look out for where
BIRTHDAY PARTIES
are on offer.
There are some excellent and unusual venues.

Places to go outside the area

Visit some exciting places just a little further afield.

BERKSHIRE

Windsor, **LEGOLAND®** www.legoland.co.uk 08705 040404, set in 150 acres of lovely parkland, offers an exciting and imaginative day out with lots of hands-on, interactive discovery. A brand new Jungle Coaster ride for 2004 promises thrills of acceleration, speed and high drops along a wild roller-coaster track that is themed to simulate an automobile test! Exciting experiences await as you wander through the Creation Centre, discover the Imagination Centre, enter LEGO® EXPLORE Land and have a go in the Driving School. Take the younger children to the Waterworks area, watch the daring stunt shows, scale the challenging Climbing Wall, brave the Pirate Falls and explore Miniland, made from over 35 million LEGO® bricks. Open 20th Mar-31st Oct, daily (except some Tues, Wed in Spring & Autumn), from 10am, closing times vary. Schools Price G **Check out page 46.**

HAMPSHIRE

Liphook, **Hollycombe Steam Collection,** www.hollycombe.co.uk 01428 724900, is one of the world's largest working steam fairgrounds. The wide variety of Edwardian steam-powered attractions provides family entertainment in a rural setting, giving an insight into different aspects of Britain's heritage. Working steam-driven exhibits include a spectacular galloper's roundabout, the ever-popular Haunted House, three railways, traction engines and rare swingboats once common in fairgrounds. Fairground organs and sidestalls help create the cheerful atmosphere. Farm animals such as shire horses are certain to appeal to younger children. Many lovely walks are available, as are light refreshments, together with an excellent picnic area. The inclusive entrance fee entitles you to an unlimited number of rides. Open all Easter weekend, Suns and Bank Hols, 4th Apr-10th Oct (daily, 1st-30th Aug), 12noon-5pm. Rides from 1pm. Schools Price C **Check out page 48.**

ISLE OF WIGHT

Sandown, **Dinosaur Isle**, Culver Parade, www.dinosaurisle.com 01983 404344. Enter a 'Pterosaur' shaped building and discover unique dinosaur relics, sounds and even smells! Take a trip through the fossilised time tunnel, stepping back 125 million years, and see life-sized dinosaur models including an Animatronic Neovenator. Guided Fossil Walks can be pre-booked (additional charge) and are usually held in high season and school holidays, or by pre-arrangement for schools. Activity sheets and a Teacher's Guide are available and there are Guided Talks and a Fossil Identification Service. In the Education Room there are themed displays at various times throughout the year. Open daily, Apr-Oct, 10am-6pm, Nov-Mar, 4pm. Schools **Open all year** Price B **Check out page 44.**

KENT

Groombridge, **Groombridge Place Gardens and Enchanted Forest,** on B2110, off the A264 www.groombridge.co.uk 01892 863999/861444. Visit the traditional walled gardens set against a 17th century moated manor or take the high level walkway through the Enchanted Forest and let your imagination run wild as you find the giant swings, gypsy camp, totem pole, Celtic ponds and many other mysteries hidden in the Forest. Then take a peaceful canal trip back to Groombridge Place. See peacocks, giant rabbits, a zeedonk and other animals. There are daily flying displays with birds of prey, including owls and an eagle. Light snacks and refreshments are available from the restaurant, and there is a shop. Open daily, Apr-Oct, 9.30am-6pm (or dusk if earlier). Schools Birthdays Price C **Check out page 48.**

42-foot-drop, abrupt twists and wild 180-degree turnarounds.

LEGOLAND® Windsor's new roller coaster is the fastest ride in the Park, topping speeds of 26mph while zipping along 1,300 feet of steel track. It also has the highest drop of any other attraction in the Park, towering nearly five stories above the ground. The attraction was designed after one of the popular LEGO® toy lines and is themed to stimulate an automobile test track while riders experience accelleration, breaking and maneuverability.

£5 OFF ENTRY

LEGOLAND
WINDSOR

V200225

2004 Opening Dates - 20th March - 31st October
Information and booking Number 08705 040404
For more information visit www.legoland.co.uk

Hever, **Hever Castle and Gardens,** www.hevercastle.co.uk 01732 865224. This enchanting 13th century double moated castle, once the childhood home of Anne Boleyn, is perfect for a day out for the whole family. The castle, magnificently restored by William Waldorf Astor, contains many treasures. The Long Gallery has an exhibition featuring Henry VIII and his six wives in full Tudor costume. Outside there is a spectacular lake, a traditional yew maze, a unique water maze and an adventure playground. Visitor facilities include two self-service restaurants, gift, book and garden shops. Ring for details of special events, including archery and jousting displays. Guided tours and information packs available for schools. Open daily from Mar-Nov. Opening times, Apr-Sept, Gardens 11am-6pm, Castle 12noon-6pm, Mar and Nov only, Castle 11am-4pm. Schools Price C **Check out page 48.**

Tonbridge, **Wear 'M' Out Children's Indoor Play Centre,** Medway Wharf Road 01732 369500. This is a family run business that prides itself on providing a friendly and enjoyable atmosphere. There is a vast play area for under 12s (height restriction 1.5m) with a selection of activities including a 19 metre Astra slide, ball pools, runways, swings, ramps and chutes, and a ride on the new Double Wave slide. There is also a separate area for under 5s and a cafe area for parents to relax and children to cool down. An adult must remain on site at all times whilst using the Centre and children must wear socks. All abilities are catered for and children with special needs are very welcome. Open daily, 10am-6pm. Birthdays **Open all year** Price A **Check out page 49.**

TRAVEL GAMES

Each choose a colour. Count how many vehicles of your chosen colour you see in a given time. Or the first one to reach ten.

Variations - This can also be played by choosing a number. Score 1 point for each number seen on a plate. If the number is repeated once on the same plate score 5 points and if 3 occur score 10 points. Either play with a time limit or the first to reach 20.

SURREY

Dorking(near), **Partytank,** Roothill Lane, Brockham, www.partytank.com Freephone 0808 100 8265, is a new concept in action adventure parks. Set in beautiful countryside, over 5s can ride the Tank Destroyer, Crazy Jeeps and the awesome Off-Road Truck. Or try archery, shoot air sniper rifles and zap the alien at the paintball range. Fly round on the Safari Ride, and get to grips with the BB machine guns and much more. Over 7s can drive quad bikes, while over 11s can have a mini-driving lesson. There is a large games area for all age groups. Entry is free on all non-show days (most Saturdays) and most Sundays there will be a variety of spectacular shows and attractions. These will include skydivers, stunt motor bike displays, an escapologist, pony riding, hovercraft, fair ground rides, car crushing with the tank, and raffles with big prizes. All activities are on a flexible token system for a whole day's fun. There is a separate site for parties, open outside the dates shown below. Open 16th May-11th Jul, 11th-26th Sept, Sat, Sun and Bank Hols; Sat, 11.30am-6pm, Sun, 10am-5pm. Schools Birthdays Price D/E **Check out inside back cover.**

Places to go outside the area

47

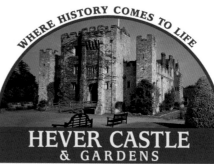

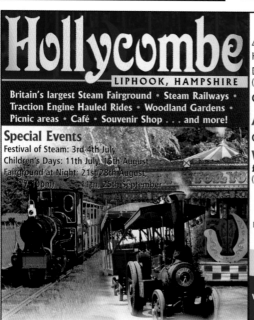

Farnham, Birdworld and Underwater World, Holt Pound, www.birdworld.co.uk 01420 22140, in lovely landscaped grounds off the A325, is well worth a visit to see beautiful birds from all over the world, farm animals, exotic fish, creepy crawlies and more. Wander around the aviaries and themed areas to see a rich variety of shapes, sizes and colours. Be sure to see the amazing Toucan beak and find out how Hornbills nurture their young. Meet some friendly birds in the Heron Theatre and find out how an owl can fly silently when a pigeon makes so much noise. Join the Birds of Prey tour, watch the penguins feeding and visit Jenny Wren's Farm for an Animal Encounter (weather permitting). Don't miss the special event days and activity weeks throughout the year, particularly in school holidays. The enthusiastic Education Team ensure you have great fun learning from all the information and activity here. There are play areas and refreshment points throughout the Park. Birthday parties are available and school parties are welcome to make use of excellent educational material. There is also an Outreach team able to visit schools. The restaurant and shop can be visited without entering the Park. Fully open daily, 10am-6pm (4.30pm in Winter) from Feb half term-end Oct, all Winter school holiday periods and weekends from Nov-Feb half term. Birdworld gardens only, open at a reduced rate, weekdays in Winter outside school hols. Combined entrance ticket to Birdworld and Underwater World and an excellent Membership scheme is available for regular visitors. Schools Birthdays **Open all year** Price D **Check out page 51.**

Guildford, Guildford Spectrum, Parkway www.guildfordspectrum.co.uk 01483 443322. Enjoy the complete leisure experience here! At one exciting venue there is tenpin bowling, an Olympic sized ice-skating rink which is home to the Guildford Flames, four pools, including a leisure pool, a 25m competition pool, teaching pool and diving pool. Other facilities include, a soft play area, laser sports game, health and fitness suite, sports arena and athletics stadium. There is a choice of catering on site and children's holiday activities are organised. Family tickets and special public sessions available. **Check out page 50.**

Guildford Spectrum offers you

A whole day of Family Fun

SWIM SKATE BOWL

Ice Skating, Tenpin Bowling or Swimming in the Leisure Pool

ALL activities for **ONLY £40**

ANY 2 activities for **ONLY £30**

Choose any 2 of these 3 activities for £30.00 (family of 4, maximum 2 adults) or 3 activities for £40.00.

Individual tickets are also available, Juniors can enjoy 2 activities for £7.30 or 3 activities for £9.90.

Family Fun tickets available 7 days a week, May 1st - Dec 31st 2004.

Your last activity must be started before 5pm.

Please call 01483 443322 for facility opening and session times.

www.guildfordspectrum.co.uk

GUILDFORD
SPECTRUM
LEISURE COMPLEX

Beautiful birds in beautiful gardens, also The Jenny Wren Farm and Underwater World.

SPECIAL HOLIDAY EVENTS PROGRAMME

Don't miss our special programme of fun days and activity weeks!

Tuesday 6th April
Easter Egg Hunt

1st - 4th June
Farm Fun Activity Week

27th July
Teddy Bear's Picnic

2nd - 6th August
'Life on the Ocean Waves' Activity Week

Tuesday 17th August
Wild West Fun Day

23rd - 27th August
'Get Wild' Activity Week

Autumn Half Term
Halloween activity week

THE LARGEST BIRD PARK IN THE U.K.

There'll be lots of fun, face painting, various entertaining workshops and much much more! Ring us nearer the dates for more details!

www.birdworld.co.uk Email: bookings@birdworld.co.uk

Birdworld, Holt Pound, Nr Farnham, Surrey, GU10 4LD Telephone: 01420 22992

LET'S VISIT LONDON

BBC Television Centre Tours, Wood Lane, Shepherd's Bush, www.bbc.co.uk/tours 0870 6030304. Discover the history, the here and now as well as the digital future, of the most famous TV Centre in the world. Thousands of programmes are produced here every year including favourites such as Top of the Pops, Blue Peter, Parkinson and CBBC. On your tour you are likely to see into studios, visit BBC News, enter into the Top of the Pops Star Bar, play within the interactive studio and much more. Tours run 6 times a day, Mon-Sat and last for up to two hours. Tours are available for anyone over the age of 9 yrs and must be pre-booked. Television Centre is a working building so studio activity on the day of your visit cannot be guaranteed. The nearest Tube Station is White City on the Central Line. Schools **Open all year** Price C.

Kew Gardens, www.kew.org 020 8332 5655 (24 hour information line). Explore Kew's spectacular gardens and see the world! Go on a journey from jungle to desert in the magnificent glasshouses, find the giant waterlily or watch piranhas swimming through the Marine Display in the Palm House. Step back thousands of years and follow the sights, scents and sounds of plant life through time in the exciting Evolution House. Visit the Museum with a fascinating interactive exhibition 'Plants+People' highlighting the importance of plants to mankind. Find the Minka house and the Pagoda, or let your senses guide you in the Secluded Garden. Hop on the Kew Explorer bus for a fun way to tour round the gardens. Children's activities, themed displays and seasonal festivals are held throughout the year. Fantastic places to eat and shop. Easy to reach on the district line tube, or by train or car. Children under 17 are admitted free. Open daily from 9.30am. Closing times vary throughout the year. Schools **Open all year** Price B **Check out page 52**.

The London Aquarium, County Hall, Westminster Bridge Road, www.londonaquarium.co.uk 0207 967 8000 (information) 020 7967 8007 (school bookings). One of Europe's largest displays of aquatic life with over 350 species in over 50 displays, including the huge Pacific and Atlantic tanks. Information on the exciting daily feeds and talks can be found on the activities screen on arrival. Includes the spectacular Atlantic dive, where divers hand feed six foot long conger eels, rays and sharks. Educational tours and literature are available. Open daily, 10am-6pm (extended to 7pm in main holiday periods). Close to Westminster tube and Waterloo tube/mainline stations. Schools Birthdays **Open all year** Price C **Check out page 56**.

London's Transport Museum, Covent Garden Piazza, www.ltmuseum.co.uk 020 7565 7299 (recorded information), 020 7379 6344 (education service), using imaginative and dynamic displays, takes you on a fascinating journey through time and recounts the story of the interaction between transport, the capital and its people from 1800 to the present day. Look out for the under 5s funbus, try the bus and tube simulators, meet characters from the past, see models and working displays and get interactive in the many 'KidZones'. More fun learning than you would have thought possible! Good educational material and lots of special holiday activities. There is now free admission for children under 16. Open daily, 10am-6pm, but 11am-6pm on Fridays. Schools **Open all year** Price B **Check out page 54**.

National Maritime Museum, Royal Observatory & Queens House, Greenwich, www.nmm.ac.uk 020 8312 6565. Dive into the largest maritime museum in the world to discover all about the past, present and future of the sea! At the Royal Observatory you can explore the solar system, the telescope gallery and stand across the Prime Meridian Line where East meets West. Open daily, 10am-5pm. (Closed 24th-26th Nov.) Schools **Open all year** Price F **Check out page 52**.

LET'S TAKE A TRIP

On the River Thames with City Cruises, www.citycruises.com 02077 400 400. Add excitement for the children, a new perspective for everyone and get excellent value by seeing some of London's best sights from the River Thames aboard a City Cruises luxury river-liner using a River Red Rover ticket! You can travel as far as Greenwich to see the Cutty Sark. For just £8.70 for an adult ticket, £4.35 for a child or just £23 for a family ticket, you can use a hop-on hop-off service between the major destination piers on the River! From Westminster Pier services run every 20 minutes to Tower Pier, and, every 40 minutes to Greenwich via Waterloo and Tower Pier. Your River Red Rover will give you unlimited daily travel between these piers. Admire the Houses of Parliament, Big Ben and the London Eye, see St Paul's Cathedral and look out for the Tate Modern. Lots to see from these super boats with cafe style facilities and a capacity of 520 seats. **Open all year** Price C **Check out page 54.**

The Original Tour, London Sightseeing Bus Tours, www.theoriginaltour.com 020 8877 2120, provides a great way to introduce children to the splendid sights of London. The open top buses afford clear uncluttered views from a comfortable seat. You can hop-on and off at over 90 easily accessed stops. Children are both entertained and educated by the special commentary designed for them, as magical stories about London unfold with tales from Roman times until the present day. Listen out for the ghostly 'Spirit of London'. There is an exclusive 'Kids Club' too. The service runs frequently, seven days a week. Times vary seasonally for each route. Every customer is eligible for a free Thames River Cruise! For more information or to enjoy a special discount call 020 8877 2120 or visit www.theoriginaltour.com and quote LGWC. **Open all year** Price G **Check out page 54.**

LET'S PLAY

Snakes and Ladders, Syon Park, Brentford, www.snakes-and-ladders.co.uk 020 8847 0946, is well signposted from Syon Park or can be accessed via 237 or 267 bus from Kew Bridge BR or Gunnersbury Underground Station. Children will find action packed fun whatever the weather. They can let off steam in the giant supervised indoor main play frame, intermediate 2-5s area or toddlers area and use the outdoor adventure playground when the sun shines. A mini motor-bike circuit provides an exciting additional activity, while parents can relax in the cafe overlooking the play frame. Open daily, 10am-6pm. All children must wear socks. Schools Birthdays **Open all year** Price A.

LET'S GO TO A CAFÉ

The Clay Café, 8-10 Monkville Parade, Finchley Road, Temple Fortune, www.theclaycafe.co.uk 020 8905 5353, is an exciting blend of cuisine and entertainment that positively welcomes families with children of all ages. The combination of a full service bistro style restaurant plus a paint-it-yourself ceramic studio offers a fresh and innovative approach to providing creative relaxation for both adults and children alike. Choose from over 200 pieces of pottery (dinnerware, vases, animals etc) and a qualified Art Technician will assist you in creating a unique masterpiece! Glass painting and T-shirt painting are also on offer. Open daily, Mon-Fri, 11am-10pm, Sat, 10am-11pm, Sun, 11am-10pm. Schools Birthdays **Open all year** Prices vary.

The Rainforest Cafe, 20 Shaftesbury Avenue, Piccadilly Circus, www.therainforestcafe.co.uk 020 7434 3111, brings the sights and sounds of a tropical rainforest into a 340-seat restaurant spanning three floors. Foods have wonderfully exciting names and there are many special effects including tropical rain showers, thunder and lightning storms, cascading waterfalls, rainforest mists and the cacophany of wildlife noises! Look out for tropical fish, chattering gorillas, trumpeting elephants, slithering boa and life-sized crocodile! Reservations possible at certain times with the exception of weekends and school holidays. Open Mon-Fri from 12noon, weekends and holidays open from 11.30am. Schools Birthdays **Open all year** Price G **Check out page 58.**

OCEANS OF COLOUR

From sharks, stingrays and
piranhas to moray eels,
lionfish and sideways walking
crabs, London Aquarium
is full of surprises with
350 different species
to discover.

Located in County Hall, right
next to the London Eye, the
London Aquarium is just over
Westminster Bridge from
Big Ben and the Houses of
Parliament, and a short walk
from Waterloo station.

So, don't plan a day out in
London without visiting
London's only Aquarium!

Check out our special group,
family and school rates.

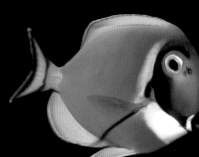

LONDON
AQUARIUM

FLOOD YOUR SENSES

Tel 020 7967 8000   www.londonaquarium.co.uk

LET'S GO TO THE THEATRE

The Lion King, Lyceum Theatre, Wellington Street, www.disney.co.uk/MusicalTheatre 0870 243 9000 (ticket hotline), 020 7845 0949 (group bookings). One of the most successful Disney films in history, stunningly recreated on stage, is a thrilling and original musical which brings a rich sense of Africa to the stage through a medley of exotic sights and sounds. The show opens in the well loved Disney setting of 'Pride Rock' where 'Simba' the new lion cub is presented to a magical parade of Safari animals. One cannot fail to appreciate the inspiration that allows the giraffes to strut, the birds to swoop and the gazelles to bound. This initial spectacle is breathtaking as the entire savannah comes to life. Wonder at the creativity of the set as the sun rises, savannah plains sway, cattle stampede, drought takes hold and starry skies give up their secrets. Huge variety is offered in the musical score ranging from pulsating African rhythms to contemporary rock. Tim Rice and Elton John's Oscar winning work is unforgettable. A show not to be missed. **Open all year Price G Check out below.**

The Miz Kids' Club, is an exciting drama experience for children to go behind the scenes of the brilliant musical, Les Misérables, and to enjoy a matinee performance of the show. This is a great opportunity for children to enter the world of theatre and discover the fascination of a big West End production. Back stage, children see the costumes and props, hear the story of Les Misérables, learn one of the famous songs, join in drama games and improvise a key scene. Older children look at the technical operation of the stage effects and focus on characterisation in their improvisation workshop. The clubs meet before the Saturday matinee at 10.30am for 8–11s and 10.45am for 12–15s, both finishing at 1.15pm. Packages, from £23, include a CD synopsis of Les Misérables, sent in advance of their visit, a snack packed lunch and a ticket to the performance on the day. For details visit www.lesmis.com or call 020 7439 3062. **Open all year Check out page 60.**

LGWTC

A WILD PLACE TO SHOP AND EAT ®

Combine animated wildlife and special effects.
Add phenomenal food made from the freshest ingredients and you've captured the breathtaking, dynamic features that embody Rainforest Cafe.

FREE
SMOOTHIE OR DESSERT
With every main course ordered by your party

020 7434 3111

20 Shaftesbury Avenue, Piccadilly Circus, London W1D 7EU
www.therainforestcafe.co.uk

Please present to your safari guide when seated.
Cannot be used in conjunction with any other offer.

Index